INVISIBLE OR INVINCIBLE
Your Choice

INVISIBLE OR INVINCIBLE

Your Choice

ROBIN H. MILLER, MD MHS

TRIUNE INTEGRATIVE MEDICINE
2022

This book is dedicated to all the wonderful women in my life who have and continue to inspire me; my patients, my family and my friends.

Contents

FOREWORD

This book is for all the women over 60 who may have felt invisible as they are aging. In *Invisible or Invincible*, I share my personal experiences and insights and present the idea that, regardless of how you are viewed by society, you have a tremendous amount of knowledge and wisdom to offer to your families and society in general.

I hope you will be inspired, no matter how old you are, to move proudly in the world and offer your gifts even if others stand in your way.

Don't let them stop you.

Walk around them and continue your path undeterred.

"Life itself is the proper binge."
— Julia Child

INTRODUCTION

YOU ARE INVINCIBLE (NOT INVISIBLE!)

*There have been many times in my life
when I have felt invisible.*

It is frustrating, unpleasant, and it hurts. I don't like that, so I have found ways to turn it around. Here is an example. Several years ago, I was part of a wine tasting weekend with some male wine experts. One was a renowned chef from Alaska, another an esteemed food and wine writer from New York, and several were avid wine collectors. Along with my husband, I spent an entire weekend of meals and tastings where these men pontificated and puffed out their wine-loving chests and never cared for my input or opinions. I was ignored, and invisible. In fact, I checked myself in the mirror to make sure I wasn't wearing an invisibility cloak!

The final celebration of the weekend was a wine dinner prepared by a local restaurant. The wines poured were old, fancy ones, placed in brown bags so the group had to identify them by taste. Frankly, the whole wine tasting thing really wasn't something I cared about. I got so fed up with the group's arrogance and their total dismissal of me, that I decided to do something about it.

I asked the weekend's organizer to tell me ahead of time the name of the final, most expensive and exclusive wine. He was happy to pull off a prank on the group. As usual, I was ignored throughout the dinner. Wines came and went and were identified. At last, the special wine of the night was poured. Each member of the "club" incorrectly identified it. Finally, loudly and clearly (since they never listened to me) I stated that I knew what the wine was. Without hesitation I said, "This is the 1981 Chateau Petrus."

They got quiet and quickly discounted my opinion. Then the wine was revealed. Of course, I was correct. They were dumbfounded, convinced they had a ringer in their midst. The organizer and I never let them in on the prank. To this day, they think I am a total wine genius. They will not forget me, of that, I am sure. Perhaps they learned not to discount people as well. One can always hope!

You might surmise already that this is not your usual medical advice book. "Why?" you ask. Because it is honest, with no holds barred, and is geared to a group of people who have been written off. I know, I am one of them. I was born in 1953. I, like many of my fellow baby boomers, am no stranger to being discounted. As I have aged, it has happened more often.

When you talk to women 60 and older, many tell you that they too feel invisible. I am here to tell you that you are *not* invisible. Rather, you are invincible! Remember the 1960s? We were young. We *were* invincible. Many protested and we were part of the sexual revolution. We changed what we could do as women. We made a difference! And then, we aged. Much of what we accomplished has been forgotten to some degree. We started to be marginalized, many of us draped in an invisibility cloak.

"How did it find its way to our head and shoulders?" you might ask. The problem is multipronged. First, we are portrayed as old in the media. Commercials aimed at us are about adult diapers and memory aid pills. We are treated as old people and vilified by society. As baby boomers, we were the change makers. We are now in the range of 67 to 75 years of age and getting older every day. We still get attention, but it is mostly negative, and we are considered a burden. We are seen as people who are bankrupting the government coffers by drawing social security, somehow undeserving of this money we let the government sock away all those years.

Retiring at record rates, our potential infirmity and possible disability present a major responsibility for those who care for us, be they family members or the government. Doctors are an especially important part of this. Unfortunately, what happens in their offices is not always helpful.

I receive phone calls from friends and family over the age of 60 telling me what happens in *their* doctor's offices. They receive little attention because they are considered old and unimportant. Pain is brushed off as the arthritis of old age, memory issues as dementia. I recently spoke to a woman in her 60s who went to her doctor because she was developing severe anxiety. Her doctor told her it was just old age setting in. He did not think anything of her 25-pound weight loss, her hyper behavior, rapid pulse, and increased blood pressure. She had hyperthyroidism. It happens to young people *and* to older people. She was written off, invisible and yet she had a totally treatable condition.

In my practice, I see countless women not misdiagnosed, but undiagnosed. Their doctors don't even try to figure out what is going on with them. They are written off as just old, often over-medicated with pain medicines and antidepressants.

Unfortunately, the fear of aging has permeated our society and resulted in the avoidance of dealing with healthy aging of our loved ones as well as ourselves. The medical establishment is no exception. Rather than finding ways to help and evaluate various ailments, it often placates and blows them off as described above.

Doctors and the public don't realize some very good news that often gets lost. There is a disconnect between what is believed and what is real.

Advances in medicine through medications, prevention, surgical treatments such as joint replacements and coronary revascularization procedures are now available to an older age group. Personalized prescription regimens help to prevent over medication. There is progress in treating and preventing dementia. Here are some examples:

> **Belief**: Severe joint pain caused by arthritis of the knee and hip create disability and lead to an early death.

> **Reality**: Joint replacement in the elderly is relatively safe. Studies back this up. Unfortunately, many doctors do not even approach the subject due to concerns that the procedures are dangerous.[1]

> **Belief**: Cardiac procedures such as valve replacement and open-heart surgery are too dangerous in the elderly.

> **Reality**: Cardiologists have developed new, less invasive procedures for aortic valve replacement known as TAVR or transcatheter aortic valve replacement. There is no need to do open heart surgery for this. It is a much safer procedure in older patients. Other cardiac procedures such as open-heart surgery have good outcomes overall in older patients.[2]

> **Belief**: Standard doses of medication work for everyone, large, small, male, or female.

     INVISIBLE OR INVINCIBLE

Reality: Simple genetic testing of medications such as antidepressants (and pain medications in the future) show that we all metabolize medications differently and that doses and types of medications must be altered accordingly.

Belief: Dementia is unavoidable as we age.

Reality: Not true! A 2001 study found that in people who are non-institutionalized, cognitive impairment between 1993 and 1998 fell from 6.1% to 3.8%.[3] In fact, according to researchers at Harvard, over the last 30 years, the incidence of dementia has declined by an average of 15% every decade in those of European ancestry living in the US. The prevalence of dementia has gone up due to the increasing number of elderlies.[4]

Great news! We are not ALL losing our minds!

There is more good news. Robyn Stone, co-director of Leading Age's long-term services and supports center of University of Massachusetts Boston, stated that as the younger baby boomers enter old age,

"the sheer numbers of older adults may help shift public attitudes."[5] In many cultures, the elderly population is revered. In our society, we are marginalized.

This is unfortunate. Our entire mindset, culturally and personally, needs to change. Just as we did in the 1960s, we are and can continue to be a force to be reckoned with.

When it comes to aging, we are our own worst enemies.

Many women buy into the idea that we should fade away. Kids growing up and leaving the house and other life changes can contribute. We often lose our identity.

Many do not pay attention to their health habits.

But as George Burns said at the age of 100,
"If I knew I was going to live this long, I would have
taken better care of myself!"

Many women slack off on healthy diets, and think they are too old to exercise. In fact, only one out of four people between 65 and 74 exercise regularly. They feel it is pointless, not realizing you can build muscle at any age. They worry about injury, but that is a lot less likely if you exercise. They are concerned they are too sick.

However, diseases such as diabetes and heart disease improve with exercise. Finally, time is an issue. However, if you are retired, you probably can find 15 to 30 minutes in your day to take a walk. AND...

What about sex?

I devoted a whole chapter to this topic. But, let me give you an important tip right now. Sex is fun and good for you at any age. Only 40% of those over 60 are having sex.

*All you wild things out there get back to your 1960s
roots. Get in touch with your rebellious selves.
It is time!*

We can redefine ourselves. This is your opportunity to find a new identity or retrieve your old one. You *can* be invincible. You are courageous, wise, and creative. Life has given you a wealth of experience to share.

In essence, you are more amazing now than you ever were. Show it!

Celebrities seem to agree. Jennifer Aniston stated at 52, "Society has put these expiration dates on us, so we need to change that. It's like…you're this age, so now is the time you go off to pasture because you're of no use to us anymore, to society. Society has some catching up to do; the language, the messaging, like we're a carton of milk with an expiration date."[6]

I am not outlining all the health issues that can affect you as you get older. For that, you might want to read the book I co-authored with Dr. Janet Horn: *The Smart Woman's Guide to Midlife and Beyond*.[7]

What I *am* doing is outlining healthy eating and behaviors that can help you feel fabulous and add to your appeal.

Many of us are incredibly productive as we age. It might surprise you to know that many superstars are 65 or older, including Rita Moreno, Jill Biden, Jane Fonda, Helen Mirren, Catherine Deneuve, Jane Seymour, and Eva Marie Saint, just to name a few.

Many people think that as they get older, there is nothing exciting or new for them anymore, but that simply isn't true. There is so much to learn and experience, regardless of how old we are.

During many years of practice as a doctor of internal medicine, I have noticed that people tend to write their own stories. These can be about what ails them or why they are where they are. However, often the stories just don't make sense or add up.

One of my favorites, which I address later in *Invisible or Invincible* is "I eat healthy." That is a good one. When I delve deeper, I invariably find that to be *not* true.

Even more amusing is, usually I am told this as they munch a hamburger and French fries. Even my own husband tries to tell me what a healthy eater he is.

That is partially true. When we eat together, he eats a healthy diet. However, at work or with his buddies, he eats all kinds of fatty foods not considered healthy. For him, I guess that doesn't count.

The other, more distressing stories I hear women tell themselves are that at a certain age we are old and of no value to society, that pain and disease are inevitable, that our health is destined to decline, and our bodies destined to age and decay.

Again, you will see, as we learn more and live longer, it is not necessarily so.

*I like Jane Fonda's take on aging. She said, "We're
still living with the old paradigm of age as an arch.
That's the old metaphor: You're born, you peak
at midlife and decline into decrepitude. A more
appropriate metaphor for aging is a staircase. The
upward ascension of the human spirit, bringing us
wisdom, wholeness and authenticity."*

You, too, can write a different story that projects health, happiness, wellness and YES, invincibility!

*As Andy Rooney stated, "It's paradoxical that
the idea of living a long life appeals to everyone,
but the idea of getting old doesn't appeal to anyone."*

As we live longer than ever, our lives need to be worth living. Unfortunately, culture, society and the systems tell women over 60 the opposite, making us feel that we cease to matter as we get older. We are treated as though we are invisible—and worst of all, too many women live their lives accordingly, as though they belong on the backburner! But I offer you a more exciting choice; to *be invincible*, not invisible. No need to let media and society define you. You are free. Redefine yourself. Write your own story. Incorporate your courage, creativity, experience, and fly! You are NOT invisible, you can choose to *be invincible*. It is just that; YOUR choice!

Invisible or Invincible shares science, stories, and personal insights which prove to us that, even though our culture may make us feel like a burden, overlooked, and unlovable, we have the opportunity to redefine who we are and live on our own terms.

Before I get into the nitty gritty, I start right off the bat with something relatively easy and can help you feel and look better. It does not cost a penny; it just takes persistence and attention. It leads me to Chapter One...The Involution Solution.

Part One

The (*Not So Basic*) Basics of Healthy Aging

1

THE INVOLUTION SOLUTION –
BONES AND HORMONES

I was lucky enough to go to Hawaii recently for a brief vacation. As I walked along the beach, I played a game with myself to try to judge how old people were from afar. I didn't ask anyone their age, but as they approached me, it was easy to get an idea of their decade.

The tell-tale sign of age was *one thing*; how they walked. It was all about their posture. I have noticed that as people age, they tend to involute; meaning, they curve in on themselves and slump. I have several acquaintances and colleagues who are in good shape, but I notice that since they have retired from their jobs, they seemed to have shrunken inward. By just standing up straight with their shoulders back, they could look 10 years younger.

As we age, some people develop a curvature of the spine known as kyphosis. But this can be corrected. A good place to start is getting coached by a physical therapist about how to stand up straight. (Believe it or not, there are even apps for that!) Having adequate muscle mass to support the bones is also important. This can be achieved with a diet rich in lean protein, plant-based foods, and healthy vitamin D levels along with adequate calcium intake.

The involution process is not only about hunching the shoulders and not standing up straight. I believe there is more to it than that. It might be a sense of not being as important without a regular job. It could be depression, or all sorts of things. I'll get to that but first, let's get physical. How do you keep your bones healthy or build them up if they are weak? Hormones can help or at least they used to.

The Women's Health Initiative study has had tremendous impact and, in my opinion, has disserviced women.[1]

Don't get me wrong, the study was well done. However, the way in which it was conducted and reported was not explained properly and caused millions of women to either stop their hormones or never start them and remain miserable during and after menopause.

Let me explain.

In 1997 a study looked at the overall health benefits and risks of hormone therapy in postmenopausal women in the US.

The researchers paid special attention to coronary artery disease, breast cancer, colon cancer and fractures. The average age of the participants was sixty-three. The women were healthy, but some were being treated for high blood pressure and high cholesterol.

Over 16,000 women with uteri still intact were enrolled to get either Premarin at the dose of 0.625 mgs daily and Provera at 2.5 mgs daily or given placebos in the form of pills that looked like the study drugs. Another 10,000 women who had hysterectomies were given Premarin 0.625 mgs alone or placebo.

With much fanfare, the study was halted in 2002, when researchers found an increase in breast cancer, heart attacks and strokes in women taking the combination hormones compared to the placebo.

The women over 65 on the two hormones had twice the rate of dementia as those given placebo.

Those on Premarin alone did not have an increase in breast cancer or heart disease but did have an increased risk of stroke compared to those in the placebo group.

Those in the 50-59 year-old age group on the hormones had less evidence of heart disease than those women in the same age group not on hormones.

There are several issues with this study; mainly that it had a dropout rate of 30% over 9 years. The women who stopped participating made up 42% of the hormone replacement therapy (HRT) group and 38% in the placebo group after a mean of 5.2 years. The study was un-blinded in 40.5% of the HRT group and 6.8% of the placebo group due to vaginal bleeding.[2] (What did they think would happen when women ten years out from menopause with intact uteri were started on hormones???) Knowing that patients were on the hormones prompted studies to search for what might happen with this type of treatment such as breast cancer and coronary disease in these patients, making it look as if the incidence was higher than it might have been.

The choice of Premarin (made from pregnant mare urine) and Provera, a synthetic progestin (not progesterone), was also a problem, in my opinion. Comparing the study results of those in the Premarin/Provera combo group to those in the Premarin alone group, it looks like Provera is the culprit when it comes to breast cancer and coronary disease. What if they had looked at natural, bioidentical estrogen such as estradiol and natural progesterone? The results would have been quite different.

A study of almost 100,000 women in France found that those on bioidentical estrogen alone had a 30% increased risk of breast cancer. However, when natural progesterone was added, there was NO increased risk of developing breast cancer. When Provera or progestin was added, the risk of breast cancer rose to 50%.[3]

What about stroke and the risk of blood clots? When estrogen and progesterone were given either in a transdermal form or under the tongue, there was no increased risk.

Why am I talking about all this when I should be telling you about protecting your bones? Because hormones do protect your bones. In the WHI study, after a 5.2 year follow up, those on hormones had a 34% reduction in vertebral and hip fractures and an overall reduction by 24% for total osteoporotic fractures.[4] Since the dramatic cessation of this study, women all over the world have either stopped their hormones or never started them. Many studies have found that this has resulted in an increase in osteoporotic fractures as well as coronary disease.

A large study utilizing an insurance data base was conducted by Islam et. al.[5] They found the risk of postmenopausal fractures increased over three years following the publication of the WHI study. It was estimated that 43,000 extra bone fractures occur yearly due to decreased HRT usage.

And a longitudinal study found that women who discontinued HRT had a higher risk of fractures compared to those who continued therapy.

Osteoporosis causes weakness of the bones and makes fractures more likely. It is estimated that ten million Americans have osteoporosis and another 44 million have low bone density. Half of all adults aged 50 and older are at risk of breaking a bone. One in two women and up to one in four men will break a bone in their lifetime because of osteoporosis. For women, this is greater than the risk of stroke, heart attack and breast cancer combined! You see where I am going with this, right?

The best ways to protect your bones is to get plenty of weight bearing and muscle strengthening exercise. Don't smoke, and drink alcohol in moderation. Get adequate calcium in the diet; for those over 60, 800 mgs is enough.

At a conference a few years ago I spoke with a top endocrinologist to find out the magic number for calcium intake. He said that most recommendations are too high. If you take too much calcium it can cause hardening of the arteries. In addition, if you take the calcium without vitamin D, it won't be incorporated properly into your bones.

Make sure you have adequate vitamin D. You will know how you are doing with a simple blood test. The sweet spot levels are between 40 ng/ml and 80 ng/ml.

Finally, if you are a good candidate for postmenopausal hormones, consider taking them. Just make sure to get them in a sublingual, vaginal or transdermal form and have your levels checked to make sure they do not go too high.

My mother is well over 85 and has been on hormones since menopause. I consider her a super-ager. She does not look or act her age. She is vibrant, smart, active and, from a distance, you would think she was 30 years younger than her biological age. Clearly there are many reasons, but the hormones contribute to her beautiful skin, her healthy brain, and her vitality. They have also protected her against colon cancer, which runs in her family. Her father, sister and two brothers all had colon cancer. She has not. This is another rarely discussed advantage of HRT. Women who have used or continue to use HRT have *half* the risk of colon cancer when compared to women who have never used them. The risk goes down the longer a woman uses HRT.

I will never forget being bullied by a male radiologist who read my mammogram many years ago. He asked why I continued to take my evil hormones. He called them poison. All I said was, if you want to see how well they work, just look at my mom! He has since involuted and retired.

2

THE MICROBIOME

To be invincible, feeling good is essential. Believe it or not, one of the main guarantees is a healthy microbiome (microbes housed in the body, such as the skin and mainly, in the gut as stool).

This brings me to the brain-gut connection. We have all experienced it. When we get nervous, we get butterflies in our stomach. When excited, we can get diarrhea. What is this connection, exactly? Your central nervous system is run by the brain as the commander. It connects with the rest of the nerves and hormones in the body. What most people don't realize is, there is also a "second brain" known as the gut. It has 200-600 million neurons and contains 90% of the serotonin in the body.[1] This is the neurotransmitter that regulates mood. Low serotonin levels are associated with depression and anxiety.

The microbiome is an important part of this connection. It communicates through the vagus nerve which ties the gut (with all its neurons) and brain together. If the microbiome is not healthy, serotonin levels will be off and the gut will leak, causing all kinds of problems. Hippocrates, the father of western medicine, stated that "all disease begins in the gut." He was probably right.

When we are born, our guts are sterile. As we develop, they are colonized with bacteria and microbes based on our exposures and genetics. These microbes provide us with a ton of benefits. They help us program our immune system, regulate our metabolism and digestion, produce vitamins and extract nutrients from our food. It is not surprising, knowing what we know about where serotonin is produced, that it also affects our overall emotional state. As early as the 19th century, an army surgeon named William Beaumont monitored gastric secretions through an opening in the stomach of a patient, created by a fistula connecting to the outside of the abdomen.[2] He noted changing moods correlated with gastric secretions. This provided a hint of the power of the gut and the microbiome.

That is why the microbiome is one of my favorite things to talk about. I present evidence for how it effects the immune system, reduces inflammation and disease, and plays a role in regulating weight and mood, and why it is so important to have a diverse and healthy microbiome, necessary to be truly invincible.

In full disclosure as someone into research who may geek out a bit, I present a variety of studies in this chapter. The descriptions and results are indented so you can skip them if you like. Either way, I provide the bottom line. Here goes.

The microbiome

Who would ever guess that the gut microbiome could be so intriguing? What is it exactly? It is the genetic material of the bacteria, fungi, protozoa, and viruses that live in and on your body.

The gene count is 200 times the number of genes in the human genome. It consists of 39 trillion microbial cells. Most are in your gut and exist in the stool. It can weigh up to five pounds. Anyone who has cleaned out for a colonoscopy and weighed themselves right after will note they lost at *least* three pounds (temporary, of course!). That was due to the literal flushing of a good part of your microbiome.

The microbiome regulates everything from the manufacture of certain vitamins and hormones, to the immune system, to the regulation of your weight and mood. Certain microbes may even protect against COVID infections. We find out more and more each year.

The microbiome is affected by various factors that include our genetics and the environment. The environmental factors have the greatest impact. Who you live with and what you eat are important factors. There are significant associations between the body mass index, cholesterol levels, waist circumference and blood pressure with the microbiome. Researchers have found that the western diet has a huge *negative* effect on the diversity of microbes, and diversity is key to a healthy gut.

The Study

To elucidate this, graduate students were given an exclusive McDonald's diet for ten days. Researchers found a significant drop in beneficial microbes in just four days.[3]

The Bottom Line

The western diet reduces the diversity of the microbiome, and it doesn't take much time for this to happen.

On the upside, to see if diversity could be *improved*, British researchers lived and ate with the Hadza tribe in Tanzania, Africa. They are considered the original hunter gatherers and have the most diverse gut microbes on the planet. The main staple is Baobab fruit, filled with vitamins, fiber, and fat within the seeds. It is also high in Vitamin C.

For snacks, they ate Kongorobi berries, loaded with polyphenols and fiber, about 20 times more than cultivated berries. For lunch they had high fiber tubers and for dinner they ate porcupine. Supposedly, it tastes like suckling pig. They also feasted on hyrax, a guinea pig-like animal with hooves.[4]

When the researchers returned home, their stool samples were tested and showed their gut microbial diversity increased by 20%, which included organisms from Africa. Unfortunately, after three days, the microbes returned to their original state. This shows that consistency with the right diet and health behaviors makes all the difference.

Diversity is important because there are distinct shifts identified in a wide variety of species that effect inflammation and several chronic diseases. It begins with the immune response. Let's start there.

THE IMMUNE RESPONSE

You might think inflammatory bowel disease (IBD) only effects younger people. However, that is not true. Ten percent of people over 60 develop IBD, including Crohn's disease and ulcerative colitis. IBD is a good example of a disorder marked by an overactive immune response to the gut microbiome. It is treated with medications that suppress the immune system. Could alteration of the gut bacteria make a difference? Possibly.

The Study

The microbiomes of 90 children being treated for Crohn's disease were studied. Those with active disease had an increase in fungus and certain bacteria that ferment lactose, such as Streptococcus, Lactobacillus, and Klebsiella. They had reduced levels of Prevotella and increased Escherichia when compared to healthy children. The treatment with antibiotics in the previous six

months was correlated with abnormal microbiota. This
may explain the correlation between the treatment of
acne and the development of Crohn's disease. Antibiotics
increase Candida and Saccharomyces. The microbiome
improved with a therapeutic dietary formula and so did
the inflammation.[5]

The Bottom Line:
Antibiotics are disruptive to the microbiome, and it
improves along with the immune response when replen-
ished with a therapeutic dietary formula. As we age, we
are more likely to receive antibiotics as our immune systems may be diminished and more likely to go haywire;
even more reason to consider boosting the diversity of
your microbiome. Then, your immune system improves,
your ability to prevent or fight infection increases and you
are healthier and stronger overall. Yes, invincible!

IS THERE A WAY TO IDENTIFY DISEASE WITH CERTAIN MICROBIOTA?

Certain markers in the stool may be used in the future to
identify disease. For example, it turns out that the bacterium
Fusobacterium nucleatum promotes tumor growth and is found
in high levels in people with colorectal cancer.[6] In women over
60, the chances of developing this are 1 in 94. Again, having a
healthy microbiome will allow you to keep this harmful bacterium at bay.

What about irritable bowel syndrome or IBS? Many doctors
label this a psychosomatic condition. New findings may prove
it is not. It is quite prevalent, affecting 10-20% of the population
over 60 years of age. Researchers have found that those with this
condition have a reduction in their microbial diversity compared
to those without IBS.[7] There are inflammatory proteins present

in the stool of these patients that may come in handy for diagnosis in the future. Another reason to work towards having a diverse microbiome.

The Gut Brain Connection

We know there is a communication between the gut and the brain that goes both ways, so to speak. Microbial dysbiosis (or abnormalities) plays a major role in how the communication occurs.

As an example of the gut brain connection, over the last century, the ketogenic diet has been used to treat epilepsy in children and helped reduce the seizure rates by half. It is used for Autism, Parkinson's, Multiple Sclerosis and Alzheimer's disease.[8] The realization of why this diet helps is becoming clear; the microbiome is enriched by the diet and is probably the reason for improvements.

Depression is another condition common in those over 60, effecting over 18%. The Flemish Gut Flora Project has found two groups of bacteria *depleted* in depressed patients: Coprococcus and Dialister. Regardless of antidepressant treatment, the bacteria did *not* come back. Both these bacteria form butyrate, which we know reduces inflammation.[9]

The Mediterranean diet (discussed in the next chapter) promotes butyrate forming bacteria. This might explain why in one study done in Australia, it reduced the severity of depression by 45% vs. 27% in the control group.[10]

When it comes to improving the microbiome and these conditions, one option is fecal transplant. This is accomplished by healthy stool replacing unhealthy stool, usually via colonoscopy. In future, it may provide crucial treatment in those with Parkinson's and Alzheimer's, diseases more prevalent in those over 60.

INVISIBLE OR INVINCIBLE

The Benefits of Fecal Transplant

The Studies

A fecal transplant study was done in 15 patients with Parkinson's disease. When given via colonoscopy, there was marked improvement in their symptoms that, for some, lasted two years.[11]

Anecdotal evidence: A recent case reported on a woman of 90 with dementia, and found that up to a month after fecal transplant, her cognition and her microbiome had markedly improved.[12]

More anecdotal evidence: Two patients with major depression were treated with fecal transplant. They experienced marked improvement in their symptoms that lasted 2 months.[13]

The Bottom Line

As gross as it sounds, fecal transplant may indeed play a major role in the future in the treatment of chronic conditions such as Parkinson's and Alzheimer's diseases as well as depression.

What about weight loss?

This area of study is fascinating and of great interest when it comes to the microbiome. For a variety of reasons, women over 60 tend to gain weight to the tune of 1.5 pounds a year. A main reason is loss of muscle due to lack of hormones and strength training. However, the microbiome plays a role.

The Studies

Twins were studied; one twin was heavy and the other thin. They had different microbiota. When the microbiota of the thin twin was transplanted to thin and fat mice, the obese mice lost weight. In addition, the obese mice were housed with thin mice, further helping them to maintain their new slim bodies.

When looking at the microbiota of both humans and mice, the obese have an increased ability to harvest energy from their diet and have more Firmicutes and less Bacteroidetes in their gut microbiome than their lean counterparts.[14]

More diversity in microbiotas is associated with leaner weight. Faecalbacterium, Bifidobacterium, Lactobacillus, and Akkermansia were associated with more diversity and leaner individuals. A study of 49 overweight people found that an energy restricted diet for six weeks partially restored the gut to normal diversity.

When mice were treated with Akkermansia muciniphila in their diet, they lost weight and their insulin levels lowered. A study in humans showed that supplementing with Akkermansia muciniphilia decreased body weight over three months, lowered insulin levels and improved insulin sensitivity.[15]

Another study

Butyrate is a short-chain fatty acid produced in the gut by bacterial fermentation of dietary fibers such as beans, fruits, and nuts. When given orally to mice fed a high fat diet, it worked on the gut-brain connection and decreased food intake, preventing obesity. Butyrate also increases beneficial bacteria independently. A relatively easy way to increase butyrate is to **exercise.** It increases the number of butyrate forming bacteria.[16]

The Bottom Line:

The microbiome plays a role in weight loss and weight gain, exactly how much of a role is still to be determined.

Further studies will shed more light (and potentially pounds) on this and provide remedies for both in the future.

DIABETES AND THE GUT

One fifth of women 65 or older have type 2 diabetes. That is a lot of women! It is essential to find a way to control it; the key is to reduce insulin resistance and improve the cells sensitivity to insulin.

Fiber is a good way to do this. It slows absorption of nutrients and improves fermentation by microbes in the gut.

The Studies

A study of non-caloric artificial sweeteners looked at glucose tolerance. Different products (saccharin, sucralose, and aspartame) were added to the drinking water of lean mice for 11 weeks. Study of their microbiota noted a negative shift. In humans, there was a strong correlation between the use of artificial sweeteners and markers for metabolic syndrome, such as weight gain, elevated fasting blood sugars and elevated hgbA1c. Medications for diabetes such as Metformin, on the other hand, have been shown to improve the microbiota.[17]

The Bottom Line

Artificial sweeteners are disruptive to the microbiome and may do the opposite of what users intend, causing weight gain rather than weight loss. Improving the microbiome by cutting these out is a relatively easy fix.

In contrast, Metformin, a common drug used to treat diabetes, may have a beneficial effect on the microbiome along with blood sugar. This may help explain why it often causes weight loss in those who take it.

Heart disease is the number one killer of women. There are many contributing factors. However, one recently identified is a substance made in the gut by the gut bacteria. The level of this substance correlates with heart disease and stroke in a more direct way than cholesterol. I am talking about Trimethylamine N oxide (TMAO). It occurs when foods containing choline and certain other components such as L-carnitine are consumed. Elevated TMAO levels correlate directly with an increased incidence of cardiovascular disease (CVD).

The Study

A study of over 29,000 people found that consuming egg yolks increased CVD risk. With each half of an egg consumed the risk went up by 1.1% and all-cause mortality risk by 1.9%. L-Carnitine is in red meat. It is also sold as a supplement. It, too, accelerated atherosclerosis and CVD risk.[18]

The Bottom Line

When it comes to heart health, a plant-based diet is the way to go, especially for those of us over 60.

Egg yolks contain 120 mgs of choline. Beef and pork, 100 mgs per serving. Fish and chicken contain 70-80 mgs per serving. Part of improvement in heart health with the Mediterranean diet is the fact that it limits red meat and dairy. The reduction of TMAO levels explains this to some degree along with the promotion of beneficial gut bacteria.

PROBIOTICS

If gut bacteria are so important, is it possible to change an individual's make-up with probiotics? The answer: possibly.

The Study

A clinical study gave healthy adults Lactobacillus paracasei DG, a healthy microbe. It increased their fecal butyrate fourfold, a good thing, for some. People who started with high butyrate levels and then took the Lactobacillus paracasei DG had a drop in butyrate by 49%. The benefits of the probiotic depend on the individual's unique pattern.[19]

The Bottom Line

Probiotic benefits are dependent on the individual, their diet, and genetic makeup.

Prebiotics

Studies have discovered a benefit to optimizing prebiotics. These are foods or supplements not digested in the upper GI tract. Asparagus, onions, and leeks are examples of prebiotics, which stimulate beneficial bacteria growth and diversity. A diet rich in prebiotics can normalize glucose levels and reduce inflammation.

Diet and Nutrition

You can take all the prebiotics and probiotics in the world but if you eat unhealthy foods, such as refined grains, starch, and sugar, they will not help.

The Study

A study of 1106 Belgians found certain things that affect the microbiome. Richness is decreased with the use of antibiotics, osmotic laxatives, IBD drugs, and antidepressants. Cigarette smoking, alcohol and soda also affect it.[20]

The Bottom Line

The microbiome is sensitive to drugs, nicotine, alcohol, refined sugar, and soda, just to name a few. It is important to focus on keeping the microbiome healthy and avoiding unhealthy habits and drugs if possible. A healthy lifestyle is important for the strength and vitality to build a more invincible you.

A diet rich in sugar and antibiotics often leads to an overgrowth of Candida (yeast). Emulsifiers in processed food disrupt the microbiome. New studies have found that micro plastics may be one cause of inflammatory bowel disease. All this means that we need to look very closely at what we put into our bodies and our family's bodies.

Treatment of viral infection?

A recent study in Japan showed that certain people eating a healthy plant-based diet have microbes that produce a compound called ursodeoxycholate, a type of bile acid. This type of bile acid keeps the virus COVID-19 from binding to cells. Studies continue to see if this compound, which is also a medication used to treat liver disease, can be used to decrease the severity or even prevent COVID-19.[21]

In the future, I foresee a medical world in which we can tailor make pre and probiotics for each patient to help optimize health, improve the aging process, and give you the energy to do all you want to do in your invincible life!

3

Eat to your health!

I love a good story. I find most people will remember the story and thus the message that comes with it. So, I begin this chapter with one of my favorites. It is an example of courage, ingenuity, *and* invincibility. It is the story of Stamatis Moraitis, told originally by Dan Buettner, author of the *Blue Zones.*[1] It is a fascinating tale.

What is a Blue Zone?

In 2010 Dan Buettner, a National Geographic Fellow and best-selling author, found five cultures around the world with the highest concentration of people living healthfully to 100 years or older. He circled them in blue on the map and that is how they got the name, "Blue Zones." The five original Blue Zones are Okinawa, Japan; Sardinia, Italy; Nicoya, Costa Rica; Ikaria, Greece; and Loma Linda, California.

Mr. Moraitis was a veteran, originally from Ikaria, Greece. He came to the US in 1943 for treatment of an arm injury that occurred during the war. He ultimately found his way to Boynton Beach, Florida where he met his wife. He had a comfortable life. In 1976, he noted he was short of breath. He went to his doctor and was diagnosed with lung cancer. This was confirmed by multiple doctors who all agreed he had about nine months to live. He was in his mid-60s at the time. He thought about treatment to buy him a little time but decided to go back to Ikaria so he could be buried alongside his ancestors. He also figured he would save money on a funeral since it is cheaper to be buried there.

He and his wife moved in with his parents who lived on a small vineyard. His wife and mother cared for him. On Sundays, he made his way to church. His friends realized he had returned and came to visit. Every afternoon, he talked with them and drank some local wine. As time went on, he felt better. He started a garden.

Time came and went, and he didn't die. He got stronger. He was able to eat the vegetables he grew. He worked in his family vineyard, took naps, walked to the local tavern, played dominoes with his friends and time flowed. He thrived and the cancer was no longer detected.

When Dan Buettner went to visit him in Ikaria, he asked him if he was able to explain to the doctors who diagnosed him what had happened. He said he had tried, but when he returned to the US for a visit, all those doctors were dead.

Mr. Moraitis lived to be 97 (102) by his own account.

In addition to living a healthy lifestyle, Mr. Moraitis followed the Mediterranean style diet, which has been studied intensely and found to have major benefits for health, happiness, longevity, and invincibility. It is the lifestyle I recommend. As our Greek friend discovered, food is medicine. If you choose correctly, it can be the best medicine for what ails you!

What is the Mediterranean diet? It is a pattern of eating rather than a diet. It includes vegetables, fruits, nuts, legumes (beans), seeds and fish. It utilizes extra virgin olive oil, very little dairy and red meat. Basically, you eat like a Greek! Those who eat this way avoid processed foods, refined carbohydrates, sugar and unhealthy fats. They do drink red wine, but in moderation.

Why should you think about eating this way? There are many good reasons.

First, it reduces the risk of heart disease. We know that heart disease is the number one killer of men and women. Multiple studies show that this is a great way of eating for your heart. A study in 2013 followed 7,000 men and women in Spain with type 2 diabetes or were at high risk for heart disease.[2] Those who ate a Mediterranean style diet with extra-virgin olive oil or nuts had a 30% lower risk of heart events. They were not given any instructions regarding exercise. The results were reanalyzed in 2018 and were upheld despite a flaw in the study protocol.

Secondly, it reduces the risk of stroke in women. A study in 2018 observed a group of over 23,000 men and women between 40 and 77 who lived in the UK. The closer a woman followed the Mediterranean diet the lower her risk of stroke. It was reduced by 20%.[3] It did not have the same reduction effect in men.

Thirdly, the diet may prevent dementia. A review published in 2016 found that sticking to this type of eating was associated with improved cognition and a lower conversion to Alzheimer's disease.[4]

Keeping your brain intact is essential for invincibility.

A small study published in 2018 examined the brain scans of 70 people with signs of dementia.[5] Those who scored low on a Mediterranean diet pattern had more beta amyloid deposits which are seen in Alzheimer's disease, and two years later had even greater increases in deposits compared to those following the Mediterranean diet.

Fourth, if you want to lose weight, this can help. The study in Spain I mentioned found those following the Mediterranean diet had a smaller waist circumference and lost more weight than those who did not. Most people do not use calorie restriction with this pattern of eating, but if you do, you will find a more dramatic weight loss.[6]

Fifth, you can live a longer, healthier life. And, when it comes to living longer, the quality of those years is important. A 2016 study from the European Heart Journal evaluated 15,000 people from 39 countries with heart disease.[7] Those who followed the Mediterranean diet were less likely to have a stroke, heart attack or die compared to those who did not follow the diet.

Sixth, eat this way and keep type 2 diabetes away! We know the risk for this condition increases in those over 60. A group of 418 people between 55 and 80 without diabetes were studied. Those who followed the Mediterranean diet had a 52 percent lower risk for type 2 diabetes in a four year follow up period. The diet was found to improve blood sugar control in another study that reviewed 20 randomized clinical trials.[8]

Seventh, this diet is anti-inflammatory. People with rheumatoid arthritis may benefit. This diet is rich in omega 3 fatty acids found to have an effect against inflammation in autoimmune diseases.[9]

Eighth, what about cancer? It reduces the risk! As we saw with Mr. Moraitis, it made a difference. Granted, it wasn't just the diet with him but, it was a big contributor. A meta-analysis of 83 studies was published in 2017. It found that the diet may reduce the risk of breast and colorectal cancer.[10]

Another study discovered that women who ate a Mediterranean diet with extra-virgin olive oil had a 62 percent lower risk of breast cancer than those in the control group eating a low-fat diet.[11]

Last, but not least, the Mediterranean diet can help depression. A study published in 2018 analyzed 41 observation studies. The diet was associated with a 33% lower risk of depression when compared to a diet rich in processed meats, sugar, and trans-fat.[12]

When you look at its core, the Mediterranean style is just healthy eating. It is about whole foods, lean protein, avoidance of processed meats and sugars, and it makes sense. The beauty is, you really don't need to count calories, just pay attention to the quality of the food you are putting into your body.

When it comes to healthy eating there is something more you can do. We now have ways to see genetically how you process different medications and if they will work for you. When it comes to eating, we can do the same thing for food. "What?" you ask.

This is cool. It is a test that looks at how you metabolize certain foods and if they are a problem for you. The one I have used is Vitagene.com. For information on the most up to date tests, check out my website: triunemed.com.

This is a simple gene test done with a cheek swab. It costs under $100 and can be purchased at Vitagene.com. It will tell you if you are a slow metabolizer of carbs and/or fats, meaning you hold on to them and the calories they contain. It can tell you if you have or are prone to lactose intolerance. It can even tell genetically if you have celiac. There are many other things the gene test can tell you in addition to the best eating plan for you as a unique individual.

The gene test explained why I gained weight on the Atkins diet, the low-fat diet, and every other kind of ridiculous diet I ever tried. The bottom line is that if I stick to lean protein and vegetables, legumes and fruit and whole grains, I can maintain a healthy weight. As you might have guessed, I am a slow metabolizer of fats and carbohydrates!

So now you know the key: stick with healthy foods and know your genetics. For weight loss, the Mediterranean style diet with calorie restriction is effective. One more tip that comes from the Blue Zones is to stop eating when you are 80% full. This is called Hara Hachi Bu. My husband who, as I mentioned earlier, thinks he is a healthy eater (NOT), does not follow this philosophy. He eats until he is stuffed. We call him Hara Hachi Bu Bu!

Getting back to what I mentioned in the beginning of *Invisible or Invincible* about the stories we tell ourselves…a big one is that after menopause, weight gain is inevitable. Even though most women think this is true, studies have disputed this. It can be combated by making muscle.

Muscle can be increased easily with strength training and healthy dietary changes. I have seen over my many years of practice that, any kind of change is difficult. Even when that change can make a difference in overall health and wellbeing, it is hard for people to do. Let me give you an example.

I had a patient with rheumatoid arthritis. She was overweight and eating foods that were high in carbohydrates. Worst of all, she was addicted to Coke (the Real Thing!). When she begged me for a "natural" solution to her inflammatory condition, I explained the importance of an anti-inflammatory diet. She balked a little, but when I told her she had to stop drinking Coke, she just couldn't do it. It took extreme pain and desperation for her to finally give it up.

Many people try to convince me that they have switched to an anti-inflammatory diet as discussed above, and I do believe they do it occasionally. But they don't get that it is a full-time deal! Fitness and health are key to getting the most out of your life. Finding a way to reclaim your health and power will help you reach your full potential of invincibility.

4

EXERCISE – DO IT THE BLUE ZONE WAY

As people get older, they tend to think they no longer need to exercise. That is how the invisibility cloak takes over. It turns out that just one out of four people between 65 and 74 exercises regularly.[1] They worry that they are too out-of-shape, too tired or too old for exercise. There is a sense that decline is inevitable. They feel it will be of no benefit. Furthermore, the prospect of intense exercise is overwhelming. You will see that anyone can and should exercise AND

high intensity exercise is not what is needed for healthy aging and of course, invincibility!

Let me explain. The best way to understand this is to take you to the Blue Zones. The place where Stamatis Moraitis lived in Greece is one of them.

WHAT IS A BLUE ZONE?

As I explained earlier, in 2010 Dan Buettner, a National Geographic Fellow and best-selling author, found five cultures around the world with the highest concentration of people living healthfully to 100 years or older. He circled them in blue on the map, and that is how they got the name, "Blue Zones." The five original Blue Zones are Okinawa, Japan; Sardinia, Italy; Nicoya, Costa Rica; Ikaria, Greece; and Loma Linda, California.[2]

These "zones" have certain qualities in common. Some include many things I have already mentioned, such as eating until you are 80% full, a plant-centric diet, and drinking wine in moderation. In addition, these groups have a community, a higher purpose, and put family first. When it comes to exercise, they do not go to a gym. They move naturally. They incorporate movement as a natural part of life. They walk to the store, garden, and explore nature. That is what Mr. Moraitis did.

This form of exercise is valuable. Even fidgeting is helpful. This is called *non-exercise activity thermogenesis* or NEAT.[3] It is the energy we utilize for everything we do other than sleeping, eating or sports activities. By moving all day long, people can get high "NEAT" scores. When this type of energy is *not* expended our weight as well as inflammation can go up in our body. This means that small movements throughout the day make a difference.

You have undoubtedly heard that sitting is considered to be the new smoking, and for those of you who have been doing a lot of sitting, it is time to get up and move…even fidget.

Researchers checked the inflammatory marker c-reactive protein, triglycerides, and blood sugar increases in those who achieved NEAT to those who did not. This lack of activity can cause problems quickly.

* * *

A study published by the American Diabetes
Association showed that inactivity for just one day
can cause cell processes to fail.
This lowers good cholesterol (HDL).[4]

* * *

People in the Blue Zones have higher levels of NEAT on a regular basis. They walk to their friends' and neighbors' homes. They perform physical tasks and have regular exercise routines such as tai chi and yoga.

How much is enough?

A total of two and a half hours of standing and light walking around the house or office is an adequate amount. Standing up for five minutes after every thirty minutes of sitting will make a difference.

Some other ideas include:

Purchase a sit to stand desk.

Walk after each meal.

Walk to a coworker's office or desk instead of calling or emailing.

Set your phone for a 30 second stretch and stand up for 5 minutes.

Walk around your house when talking on the phone or watching TV.

Take the stairs when you can.

Walk an hour every day.

Find an activity you like to do such as swim, run, ride a bike, dance, and try to do some form of these daily.

These activities provide a powerful strategy for exercise.

Furthermore, as we get older, we need to keep our muscles healthy. Do that with strength training.

We know that aging is associated with physiologic and functional decline which can lead to falls, disability, and frailty. The fact is that aging leads to muscle loss. However, there is a way to prevent this. The answer is strength training two to three days a week. It builds muscle strength, muscle mass, and maintains bone density. It is also good for preventing heart disease, type 2 diabetes, and arthritis.

I have trouble motivating, so I work with a trainer two days a week. I admit, I do not like it, but I do it. I know how important it is for my strength and vitality. I also keep stretchy bands in my family room to use when I watch movies or TV.

You don't need a trainer. Carry your groceries, find yoga exercises that utilize body weight, get a consultation with a physical therapist to show you how to do this on your own and then do it! When it comes to exercise, the goal is to make it a natural part of your life, something that is easy and fun to do every day.

Tale of Two Women

I just explained how the Blue Zone's method of movement works. Perhaps the best way to truly understand it is to hear the stories of two women; one who exercised her whole life and the other who claimed to be "allergic" to exercise.

Jane, born in 1930, was active her entire life. Her father died when she was young, so her mother raised her alone. She did a lot of chores around the house to help her mom. She also was able to do all kinds of fun activities. She played tennis, went to sleep-over camp in the summers where she excelled in water sports. Her activity never stopped. She went to college and got married. She had children and was busy with them; hiking, swimming, ice skating, skiing, and playing outdoor games. Once the kids grew up, she continued to play tennis and hike. In addition, she ate a plant-based diet with lean protein. She is still moving, she never stops. She is almost 92 years old and healthy and active. She is a force to be reckoned with; invincible.

Joan, born in 1929, grew up with a single mother as well. Thanks to wealthy grandparents, she was afforded private schools, went to college, and got married. She was able to hire nannies for her children. She was involved in teaching and all

                                    INVISIBLE OR INVINCIBLE

kinds of political activities. She had no time for exercise and was not active at home. She lived in an apartment in a major city and rode the elevator. She ate a diet rich in fats and processed foods. At the age of 70 her memory started to slip. She was diagnosed with Alzheimer's disease. By the age of 78, her dementia was so severe that she forgot how to eat. She died shortly thereafter.

Both women were educated. Both had comfortable lives. One was and continues to be active, the other was not. Granted, genetics may be at play to some degree, but healthy eating and exercise were the most likely reasons that Jane is still going strong, and Joan is gone.

5

ESTHETICS

The actors in the many commercials for fillers and Botox are almost always beautiful young women. However, the target market is older women. There are many who say they want to embrace their aging skin. But there are others who don't want to and that is quite OK. When it comes to looking and feeling better, you don't have to be a purist. If enhancing your beauty makes you feel good and invincible, do it! It can be empowering and give you confidence.

There are some amazing artists out there who can help to make you feel beautiful and bring your skin back to life. Once a month, I go to an esthetician for a facial. It feels great and when I finish with her, my skin glows.

I found a wonderful product called "Droplette" for in between facials. My son gave it to me as a gift. It is a little machine that drives the various skin serums below the surface. It takes 60 seconds, and it is done. There is something for the morning to give you a glow, and collagen to build up your skin, and retinol to diminish wrinkles. I have to say it is pretty amazing and they aren't paying me to write about this! All you need along with Droplette is a nice moisturizer. I have been using Skin Drink's Mushroom Trilogy serum.

If you want to go deeper, there are fillers to pump up your cheeks or your chin which can last several years. Botox diminishes wrinkles. For me, the more active I am the quicker it wears off and I can't afford to keep doing that. However, the fillers *are* nice. If you have an expert inject them, no one will know!

The greatest complement I receive after any of these treatments is that people ask if I have been on vacation recently or if I have done something different with my hair!

If you cannot use HRT due to a family history of breast cancer and you want to preserve your skin, you can apply it to your face directly. It is not absorbed into the body. I have tested patients' levels just to make sure.

I work with some very talented compounding pharmacists. It is possible to meet with the pharmacist to devise a personalized skin cream. She utilizes a variety of components and often combines vitamin C, B and E which penetrate the skin easily. They offer anti-oxidative protection. Vitamin A or Retinol also offers protection and can induce synthesis or the production of collagen. It reduces pigmentation and enhances the turnover of the overlying skin.

A healthy diet rich in antioxidants will help skin tone, as well. The foods found to promote this are turmeric, green/black tea, ginger, garlic, onion, and foods high in fiber, magnesium, vitamin D and omega-3 fatty acids. Foods rich in flavones, isoflavones, beta-carotene and flavanols are also key. Note that these are all part of the Mediterranean style diet; colorful fruits and veggies.

What you want is to promote collagen and prevent its breakdown. Sugar is the one thing that will destroy it. Hyperglycemia promotes wrinkles. So do foods that promote advanced glycation end products or AGEs.[1] These are from animals high in fat and protein, such as red meat. High fat cheeses are high in AGEs. Sugary, highly processed and prepackaged foods are also high in AGEs.

To block the AGEs, foods and spices such as cinnamon, garlic, yerba mate, cumin, ginger, black pepper, green tea, and tomato paste look promising. The important thing to remember is that you can look and feel better by adjusting your diet and lifestyle. Be invincible. You are capable, the power is in your hands. In addition, if you choose to add another path on your journey you might want to explore these many options.

———

6

———

PLASTICS WITHOUT SURGERY

Many reactions can be anticipated when the subject of plastic surgery comes up. Those into being completely natural feel it is sinful and would never try it. Others are neutral. And, many are interested or at least intrigued. Let me tell you, when executed properly by the right professionals, it can make you feel good. Sometimes women need that boost to give them confidence to find their inner strength, power, and invincibility. I describe to you a variety of things from top to bottom. Even if you are not interested in esthetics, you might be curious about benefits and risks (and costs) and what results might be expected. This in no way obligates you to do any of it. So, please read on.

FOR THE FACE AND NECK:

Let's start with Botox. We hear about it all the time. Comedians joke about it, and models swear by it. What exactly is it?

Botox is a brand name drug made with the toxin Clostridium botulinum. It is injected to relax creases and wrinkles. It is also used to block underarm sweating, muscle spasms in the throat and shoulder, spasm of the eyelids, eye twitches, chronic migraine, overactive bladder, and a type of esophageal spasm known as achalasia. It works by blocking signals from the nerves to the muscles.

Botox is given by injection and only takes a few minutes. It can take up to 14 days to see the full effect. It lasts up to 6 months but usually wears off sooner than that. If injected properly, it can help with wrinkles not just of your face, but of your neck and decolletage. I was a guinea pig/model for a friend who is a true artist and nurse practitioner. She trains other doctors and nurses to work with Botox. She injected Botox to relax my neck and decolletage muscles. It was quite amazing! I did not expect the great results.

These injections are relatively safe if performed by someone who knows what they are doing. Be aware that complications can arise. There may be mild pain or swelling and bruising at the injection site. Depending on how it is done, it can cause a droopy eyelid or a crooked smile and drooling. It is unlikely but if it spreads to the body, you can have muscle weakness, vision problems, trouble speaking or swallowing and/or trouble breathing. I have never seen any of these side effects, but I live in a community with excellent providers.

Do your research if you are considering Botox. It can help you look younger. Just be careful. Depending on how much is used, it can get expensive. Botox is measured in units and usually costs $10 to $15 a unit. An average dosage is between 30-40 units which can cost between $300-$600. If more than one area is treated, you can imagine how it adds up AND it needs to be repeated within a few months if you want to maintain the result.[1]

It is possible that Botox makes the skin more elastic with repeated use. This may help prevent future wrinkles. We will probably get to observe over time if this is the case, since more than 6.6 million Americans used Botox last year alone. It is an intriguing idea, for sure.

DERMAL FILLERS

Dermal fillers treat wrinkles on the face, as well. They plump up smile lines, lips, and cheeks and can also be used on the hands.

There are many different forms of fillers which last for varying amounts of time.

Calcium hydroxylatpatite or Radiesse is a gel solution that lasts for 18 months.

Collagen lasts for up to four months.

Hyaluronic acid is a material that loses its effect after about 6 to 12 months.

Poly-L-lactic acid known as Sculptra is a synthetic material that lasts around two years. It is very effective for a smooth look on the face and neck area. It requires a total of three treatments each about one month apart.

The one permanent FDA approved dermal filler is known as polymethylmethacrylate beads.

Again, the results can be remarkable. As we age, our skin begins to sag and our cheeks and chin kind of sink. These fillers plump those areas and can have a beautiful effect. Of course, as with anything, there are risks and, again, you need an experienced provider to inject them.

The risks include an allergic reaction, bruising, infections, numbness, itching, redness, scarring, and swelling. Inflammation of the area can occur with illness. Some women have experienced swelling with influenza infections and, it has been rarely seen with the COVID vaccine. However, these reactions are temporary.

The costs can add up depending on how much is used. Providers charge by the syringe. Usually, the cost is in the $2500 range.[2]

LASER

There are many types of laser therapies. The popular treatment of the hour is BBL or Broadband light laser therapy, also called the photo facial. It is used to treat spider veins, acne, and rosacea and helps with fine lines and wrinkles and can even out skin tone. It helps with sun damage, large pores, dull skin, redness, and sagging skin. It increases the elasticity of the skin and helps the body regrow healthy skin.[3]

Laser therapies are generally done by a dermatologist and involve multiple sessions. A session lasts around 30 minutes. A cooling gel is applied to the treatment area and your eyes are protected with goggles. It might be slightly uncomfortable, and the skin might feel warm and become slightly red and/or swollen.

BBL uses a broad spectrum of wavelengths to target the deeper levels of the skin. The skin absorbs this and promotes collagen production while eliminating pigmented cells. Changes can be seen in the skin within a few days or weeks of the first treatment. Things really start to improve after multiple treatments. Generally, 3 to 6 sessions are recommended with two treatments yearly thereafter. Several small studies have found that it is safe and helpful for reducing enlarged pores, tightening the skin, and increasing the thickness of the skin with improved collagen and elasticity.

Of course, something this good carries a hefty price tag. Depending on where you live it can cost anywhere from $4000 to $10,000.

THREADS

Special kinds of stiff threads can be inserted in the face and neck and lift the tissues. Using a basket weave pattern approach, the targeted areas are lifted. In the long term, it stimulates collagen production and provides a more youthful appearance. This is a short procedure with very little recovery time. The results are temporary and maintenance treatments are required every 6 to 12 months. Some people experience bruising and swelling.

There are various types of threads available. Over time they dissolve under the skin. If there is a problem, they can be removed. Some are barbed and may be more effective but more difficult to remove if problems arise. A reputable provider is essential. Some threads made in China can be dangerous, causing infection and scarring. It is important to use threads made and approved in the U.S.

 INVISIBLE OR INVINCIBLE

The cost depends on how many threads are used. For example, a neck "thread" lift costs about $800 and lasts about a year.[4]

MICRONEEDLING

Microneedling is aimed at stimulating collagen production and improves the appearance of the skin. It is done with a special tool that makes small pricks under the skin. It is done across the skin. It generally takes about a half hour to complete the entire face. After the procedure a serum or calming treatment is applied. It is helpful for the reduction of acne scars, age spots, large pores, and reduced skin tone. On other areas of the body, it is helpful for stretch mark and scar removal. The risks include bleeding, bruising and infection and peeling. After treatment, most people experience some redness, but recover quickly.[5]

The price varies widely, from $200 to $700.

PLATELET RICH PLASMA AND THE VAMPIRE FACIAL

You may have heard about this type of facial in fashion magazines. They have become quite popular and sound pretty gross, but they can be effective. With this type of treatment, your blood is drawn and the plasma is separated. The plasma is injected back into your skin using the microneedle. It promotes growth of healthy cells. There is little risk if done by a trusted professional. Given the other effective facial procedures available today, I think it makes little sense to do this treatment. It is expensive as well, costing between $1000 and $3000. Laser, facials with peels, and microneedling alone may be a better bet.[6]

MICRODERMABRASION

I personally like this procedure. It is painless, relatively inexpensive and you feel and look good afterwards. The procedure uses a special applicator with an abrasive surface that gently sands your skin. It does not hurt. It is good for fine lines and wrinkles, hyperpigmentation, large pores, sun damage, acne, and acne scars and stretch marks. It can be done monthly. Most dermatologists offer a package for multiple treatments. The cost varies widely from $50 to thousands depending on where you live and who is performing the procedure.[7]

Natural Facelifts with Acupuncture and Yoga

I have a an acupuncturist friend who specializes in natural facelifts.

After a total body acupuncture treatment, then comes the facial. The acupuncturist inserts 40 to 70 tiny needles to the face. It is like microneedling but these needles are less intense. The needles will stimulate the circulation and lymphatics in your facial area. They also stimulate collagen production and elasticity.

The treatment results are not as dramatic as fillers and Botox; however, most people see improvements after about five sessions. Ten treatments appear to be optimal, followed by maintenance treatments every four to eight weeks.

What about Yoga?

The yoga facelift utilizes muscles of the face in various exercises. This requires a one-hour session several times a week. Once desired results are achieved, 15-minute daily sessions are required for maintenance. The exercises improve blood flow to the face and diminish wrinkles. There is no scientific evidence that this works. Some people swear by it and others feel it could have the opposite of the desired affect causing jaw line prominence and rosacea.

Let's move on to the neck!

Erma Bombeck wrote about it in her book, *I Feel Bad About My Neck*. It wasn't until I passed 60 that I knew what she was talking about. Along with everything else, it can start to sag. That is

INVISIBLE OR INVINCIBLE

where the beauty of turtleneck tops come in! But there is a limit to how many turtlenecks you can wear. So, there are non-surgical options if, like Erma, you have neck issues!

Kybella is the latest therapy to revolutionize the treatment of the neck without surgery. It is an injectable used to melt the fat under the chin. Some people have more fat than usual under the chin, also known as a double chin; this gets rid of it. Double chins can be genetic or caused by weight gain. A study by the company that makes Kybella found that in 2015, 47% of those who think they have a double chin are unhappy about it. In the past, the usual treatment was liposuction.

Now there is Kybella, an injection that kills fat cells under the chin. It is the synthetic form of deoxycholic acid, a naturally occurring substance in the body known to break down dietary fat. It has been approved by the FDA and deemed safe. The injections should be given by someone properly certified by the manufacturer of the drug.

A trained esthetician will know how and where the injections need to be placed. The neck and chin will be numbed prior to injection. Some will receive up to 50 evenly spaced injections during a single treatment. The treatment takes about 30 minutes. Afterwards there can be swelling and slight bruising. It can take up to three weeks for this to go away, although most look normal after a few days.

Results are individual; some will only need one treatment, but the majority will need more. Some need up to six treatments administered one month apart. In fact, studies have found that 59% of patients required the full six. Results can be seen four to six weeks after the first injection, which is why it takes at least two sessions to see results. The results are permanent, there is no surgery and no downtime. It can be pricey with one treatment costing between $800 to $1200, but it isn't surgery, and that is a huge plus![8]

Radio Frequency-based devices

These devices have been around since 2001 for the use of skin tightening, under the names of Thermage and Exilis, to name a couple. These are relatively safe treatments, using energy waves at the slow end of radiofrequency ranges. It is 100 million times slower than visible light. It can produce heat that works at the deeper layers of the skin to induce new collagen and elastin growth, causing the skin to become thicker and firmer with a more youthful appearance. Since it is at a low frequency, it can safely penetrate to a deep level, helping to improve skin tone and lift tissues. This is a particularly effective treatment for the neck.[9]

Ultrasound

Ultrasound is commonly used to image parts of the body. However, it can be very useful for the skin. It can lift it and promote the production of collagen. A treatment known as Ultherapy is approved by the FDA and used to target deep tissue layers of the face and neck. It helps with skin tightening by penetrating 5mm deep under the skin and reaching the second layer of muscles underneath the facial muscles. It bypasses the outer layers and goes straight to where collagen is made. It is a good alternative to a neck lift. It takes three to six months to see the full effect. Some people may need up to three treatments. Those who have had this treatment are quite satisfied with the results.[10]

The treatment itself can be slightly uncomfortable. There is no downtime afterwards. The treatment cost averages $1700.

On to the Abdomen, buttocks, and thighs!

If you are like 90% of the women out there, you have cellulite and have no doubt wondered if there will ever be anything to get rid of it. I have been looking at and trying all kinds of creams and treatments for years and nothing really worked. Now there is something called QWO or collagenase clostridium histolyticum.

Cellulite is the dimpling of the skin around pockets of fat. It occurs when bands of collagen tether the skin to muscle. When fat is deposited between the skin and muscle, dimples form. Up until now, there have been no good treatments for cellulite. QWO, an enzyme that targets the collagen to release the banding and ultimately smooth out the skin, is changing that.[11]

The doctor performs up to 12 injections to the dimples on the affected area. Right now, it is only approved for the buttocks, but probably will be approved for other areas soon. It is usually administered three times, 21 days apart. It is non-invasive apart from the injection and requires little downtime. In clinical trials it reduced the severity of dimpling and has been very effective.

Since this is a relatively new treatment, long term effectiveness and side effects are still unknown. It does appear to be safe and well tolerated. The cost is $2900 for a total of three treatments.

I have received this treatment and am very happy with the results. Just make sure you find a skilled provider who understands the treatment and how to inject it!

Cool Sculpt

CoolSculpt or Cold Liposuction is a treatment that freezes and kills fat cells. The practitioner places applicators on the targeted areas. The abdomen, flanks, and thighs are the most commonly treated areas.

Patients usually feel a sucking sensation and then intense cold. The procedure takes about an hour with little downtime. Multiple sessions may be needed and may take months to see results. The company claims to reduce 20 to 25% of fat cells in the targeted area. It could cost $2000 to $4000, depending on the area and number of treatments.[12]

There has been negative publicity due to poor results noted by supermodel Linda Evangelista, who suffered a rare but real phenomenon that can occur post CoolSculpt. The opposite of fat shrinkage called Paradoxical Adipose Hyperplasia or PAH can occur, where the fat increases rather than decreases.

If this occurs, the company will pay for liposuction, a procedure patients were trying to avoid in the first place, but it does take care of the problem area.

In Summary

As we get older, things about our appearance and our body start to bug us. Many people can deal with this gracefully. Others would like to do something about them. There is no judgment, either way. However, remember

Billy Crystal (as Fernando Lamas) stating,
"It is better to look good than to feel good."

There is a tiny grain of truth there. Not that feeling good isn't a priority. It is. But *when* you look good you do feel good! Even if all you do is a home facial, it can make a difference. And, when you feel good you light up yourself, and those around you, and you become invincible and no longer invisible.

———

7

———

HEALTHY AGING –
CAN YOU TURN BACK THE CLOCK?

Invincibility is all about aging and how we approach it. Are we going to wither away or are we going to continue to ascend the staircase to wisdom and authenticity, as Jane Fonda stated?

Although the COVID pandemic has slightly decreased the average life span of adults in the US, it is still a possibility that half of today's 5-year-olds can expect to live to 100 years.[1] And for many women like us who are over 60, it is also possible to live to 100, but what is the point unless our quality of life is good?

Fortunately, there is a burgeoning field of geoscience (the science of aging), that will transform how we age by finding ways to reprogram genetics and molecular and cellular mechanisms that are at the root of many diseases and debilitating conditions. Whether we like it or not, they increase in frequency as we get older, but it looks more like we can do something about that. We can shape our environment to promote healthy living spaces. Many of us are retired and ready to flex our invincible muscles by becoming activists to work for these causes. It is time.

To help with this, the Stanford Center on Longevity has launched an initiative known as *The New Map of Life*, designed to meet the challenges of those who live longer. [2] They suggest that having age diversity is important for healthy aging of the entire population.

If we invest in our children and optimize health and wellness at each stage of life, we reap major benefits. We must invest in public health and address health disparities. It is important to understand that with these advances, we will be able to work more years and, in doing that, have more flexibility when it comes to hours and the workplace. In some respects, the pandemic accelerated this. With extra productive time, we can claim our power of invincibility and become lifelong learners with many educational options at all stages of our lives.

This is how we nurture and grow ourselves as we soar past 60 years of age. We can develop communities that feed our overall health; diverse age and racial populations that provide a healthy environment with clean air, water, and places to enjoy the outdoors and exercise. With this, we all prosper and thrive!

Let's talk details

To help prevent involution and invisibility, let's drill down and get specific about what aging physiologically is all about.

Is age just a number? Not always. The Stanford project discovered a protein level in the blood that can predict a person's age.[3]

With a physiological clock, they look at the level of 373 circulating proteins in the blood. The levels of these proteins may be responsible for aging.

The Study

A study was performed in 4263 people between the ages of 18 and 95. The researchers found that physiological aging does not occur at a regular pace but is more of a jerky process. They found three inflection points in our life cycle: 34, 60 and 78. This is when the proteins change. The levels of many proteins will remain steady for a while and at some point undergo an upward or downward shift. These shifts happen in young adulthood, late middle age, and old age. Using this model, the researchers were able to predict individuals' ages within a range of 3 years,

   INVISIBLE OR INVINCIBLE

most of the time. If the predicted age was substantially lower than the actual age, the reason was the person was remarkably healthy for their age.[4]

The samples from these studies came from the Longevity study, a registry of exceptionally long-lived Ashkenazi Jews, many of whom live to the age of 95. They found 1379 proteins of varying levels of the 3000 proteins studied. When they reduced them to 373, they could predict ages with accuracy. When the results between chronological age and physiological age were off, it was due to the extreme health of that group.

A good predictor in this group of a younger than predicted age was hand-grip strength and cognitive function. The study also found that men and women age differently. Of the proteins analyzed, 895 were more predictive for one sex more than the other.

The Bottom Line

The Stanford researchers identified certain proteins that predicted the subjects correct age within three years. When there was a discrepancy, it was because the person was unusually healthy or conversely unhealthy for their stated age. And...

Surprise! Men and women age differently!

What About the Brain?

When asked what worries them most, many women over 60 will say what they fear even more than cancer is losing their minds. That is why brain research is so important. Fortunately, Stanford scientists have found a key factor in *mental* aging.[5] It has to do with our immune system. Over time, for some people, the immune system goes a bit haywire. It does the opposite of what you would like and causes inflammation. This inflammation is at the root of heart disease, Alzheimer's disease, cancer, and failure to thrive in general.

The big question has been, which immune cells are the problem? The researchers think they have found them. They are called myeloid cells, found in the brain and circulatory system. They fight infection and clean up debris such as dead cells and clumps of protein. They watch for invaders. As we age, they get tired and slack off. They can get confused and adopt a new agenda and fight enemies that aren't there. The result is, they hurt innocent tissues.

In mouse studies, blocking the interaction of myeloid cells between certain hormones and receptors restored youthful metabolism. It also reversed mental decline. By adjusting the immune system, researchers de-aged the brain.

The myeloid cells create a positive feedback loop interacting with hormones and their receptors creating inflammation. They hoard glucose (sugar) instead of spending it. When the cells become energy depleted, they go into an inflammatory rage and hurt aging tissues.[6]

This process can be downshifted using a chemical compound. By blocking this hormone-receptor reaction on the surface of the myeloid cells, the cells can metabolize the sugar and reverse the inflammation. In mice, this process reversed their age-related cognitive decline. Even if the compound did not cross the blood-brain barrier, it was still able to have a positive effect. Although the compound is not toxic in mice, we do not yet know how it works in humans. Knowing the mechanism, human trials will be forthcoming.

We are one step closer to reversing the aging process of the brain and body. There is even better news when it comes to the mechanics of how we age. It is fascinating that the researchers have found certain biological pathways along which we age. They are called ageotypes.

We have known for years that certain markers, such as high cholesterol, are more common in aging populations. But what else is going on?

The Study

The researchers profiled 43 healthy men and women between the ages of 34 and 68. They took lots of blood and measurements at least five times over two years. They noted that people age along different biological pathways. These include metabolic, immune, hepatic (liver) and nephrotic (kidney). Our bodies age along these pathways. Metabolic agers are those who are at high risk for diabetes and have elevated markers of high blood sugar known as hemoglobin A1C and blood sugar levels. Those with an immune ageotype might have higher levels of inflammatory markers and be prone to immune-related diseases. A single individual can have several aging processes going on at once. If this happens, it is possible for the individual to reverse these markers and decrease or even reverse aging. For instance, lowering hemoglobin A1C by improving their diet and exercising, reducing inflammatory markers with diet, stress management, and exercise can do it. What is very interesting is that they looked at the differences in aging between healthy participants and those who were insulin resistant. There were 10 molecules that differed significantly between them, and those markers were involved in immune function and inflammation. By modifying lifestyles and reducing sugars, the team saw aging markers *decrease.* This occurred not only in hgbA1c levels and inflammatory markers, but in kidney function as well.[7]

The Bottom Line

Modifying your lifestyle and diet *can* decrease your markers for aging. In other words, you *can* lower your physiologic age.

Different systems age at different rates.
You can improve your ageotypes
by living your best invincible life.

Further evidence

The shortening of chromosomes, your DNA, is associated with aging. A 2021 study found that physical exercise (aerobic and/or endurance) is most effective when it comes to conserving intact chromosomes. This confirms the idea that you can slow down or even possibly reverse the aging process.

     INVISIBLE OR INVINCIBLE

AND, ONE MORE THING!

When it comes to lifestyle changes it is not just important to exercise and eat well. Having passionate activities can have a huge influence on well-being and aging. Adding playfulness can also help. Pennsylvania State University studied the relationship between healthy aging and playfulness.[8]

Fifteen qualities they identified were being happy, optimistic, cheerful, joyful, positive, relaxed, enthusiastic, mischievous, naughty, clowning, teasing, creative, whimsical, funny, and humorous. They postulate that adult playfulness is an important characteristic of cognitive function and emotional growth in aging. My personal experience with this is witnessing my mother who has all fifteen of the qualities and is sharp as a tack.

Hence, the choice of invincibility over invisibility (unless, of course, she is mischievously sneaking through a fence to exercise in a high brow neighborhood). What is key is to find your proper mindset.

PART TWO

THE INVINCIBLE MINDSET

$$8$$

Personal Views on Aging

Like most people, I never thought much about aging when I was young. As I grew up, attended medical school, and did my residency training, I still didn't think about it much, at least for myself. I just saw older people as those who needed my care and who typically took *way* too much work. We even had a term for the older women who showed up at the hospital. The term was LOL in NAD (This was well before the concept of emojis...when LOL became Laugh out Loud!). The interpretation: "little old lady in no acute distress." At the time, they were probably women 60 years and older. Now I am that age and I absolutely do not think of myself as a LOL (little old lady)!

Like patients I used to see, I am beyond Medicare age, and I can't even think about applying for it. Fortunately, I have medical insurance through my husband's company. So, I suppose I fight the concept to some degree. In my head I am in my 40s.

Each decade of my life so far we have celebrated my birthday with a family party. I look forward to them. My 60th birthday was no exception but for another reason.

I had a wonderful, funny, spunky friend. At 50, she was diagnosed with ovarian cancer. She kept it at bay for five years. Talk about seizing life and taking it for all a person could! She did everything the doctors suggested in terms of therapy. Knowing that her odds were not great even with treatment, she traveled extensively. She wrote letters to her children so they could read them when they experienced life events in the future.

She was divorced and right about the time she was diagnosed, she found her soulmate. Even knowing that she was dying, she had a commitment ceremony with him. It was a beautiful event; a way to let him know how very much he meant to her. She met many women her age or older who bemoaned how old they were and complained vociferously. She never said anything to them. However, in our discussions she told me how she would love reach their age if she could.

She made it to my 60th birthday party. Right beforehand she told me again that she was envious. She would have been thrilled to make it to *her* 60th birthday. Sadly, she died a few months after the party. Nothing like confronting mortality to help form a person's views on aging.

After she died, and I saw all she went through, I focused on appreciating every moment. I think of her often. You never know what is ahead. Life can turn on a dime.

I have taken care of many people over the years. It is remarkable how random certain life changing events feel. I remember caring for a woman in her early 60s who, late in the evening, presented with abdominal pain in the area of her spleen. The weird thing was, it was throbbing. It turned out she had a dissection, or split, in the lining of her aorta, the main artery of the body. It couldn't be fixed; it was too extensive.

She had a great life with a husband who adored her. When he brought her in to the hospital where I examined her, he had no idea she wouldn't be going home with him. All the couple could do was hold each other until she died. She was fairly lucid till the end. It was tragic and so sad. All *I* could do was cry with them and comfort them both. That morning was like any other day until the pain struck. Their story is an example of why it is so important to live every moment and appreciate the people in your life, just as my friend did when she realized her life was being cut short.

It is important to be as healthy as you can, and I vowed to do that as I have aged. Fortunately, I have an excellent role model, my mother. She is amazing. She has always eaten a healthy, red meat free diet. She exercised her entire life. She was passionate about her work as a psychiatric social worker. When she retired, she continued to keep her brain and body active and do all the screenings recommended. She still does. She is vital, active, and looks 20 years younger than her actual age. She is what is known as a super-ager.

Following her example, I quit eating red meat 20 years ago, try to stick to a Mediterranean style diet, and keep my mind active. I do my requisite health screenings. I meditate twice daily, and I choose activities I am passionate about. I exercise regularly and watch my weight. I try my best to age gracefully. Even though I am a doctor, I do my best to avoid them.

Earlier in *Invisible or Invincible* I offered to help with both feeling and *looking* good as we age.

The term anti-aging is distasteful to me because it is not something you can fight. Aging is inevitable. I believe healthy aging is where we need to put our focus.

Culturally, at least here in the US, aging is viewed as the enemy and the elderly are not appreciated. How weird that something we all experience is so feared and vilified. How did we get this way?

Read on.

9

Cultural Views on Aging

It is clear from adult diaper and memory supplement ads that we live in a society where reaching 60 years and living beyond is not seen as a vital stage of life. Perhaps that is why so many fear it and why many young people have trouble facing their aging family members. In the media, this older age group is most often ridiculed and joked about. There have been a few serious shows and movies about aging, but for the most part, we are hidden and, yes, invisible. Heck, even those suggestive Viagra ads show women in their 20s talking about how well it works. And Botox ads present young women as well.

Many studies have addressed the cultural views on aging in the US to understand it and effect positive change. What most have found is that life satisfaction tends to decline as we age but is not inevitable. The good news is that there has been some improvement in well-being (physically feeling good) as we age. However, the sense of being fully engaged in life and having purpose often takes a downhill plunge from midlife and beyond here in the US.[1]

Historical perspective on age and ageism

Full blown ageism, prejudice against the elderly, is "sort of" a new concept. Think about it. In 1900, the life expectancy of women averaged 43. Most did not get old. At that time, those who did live to be older, were respected for their survival skills, their information and advice. At that time, families tended to live together and care for each other.

However, ageism got its roots long before, contributed to by two major events in history. The printing press, invented around 1440, improved literacy which made story telling less necessary. The industrial revolution from 1760-1840 promoted youth and vitality and made some older workers obsolete. As life expectancy increased with new advances in medicine and science, younger people felt the drain on their resources from caring for their elders.

Then ageism really took off. The nuclear family scattered as children left rural areas and moved to cities for good jobs.[2]

Ageism continues with the perpetuation of myths/beliefs and misconceptions. Here are some examples:

Belief: Older citizens are unproductive.

Reality: We are living and working longer. Even those who have stopped working often become volunteers (25%) or help their families (6%).[3] I've had many patients who are raising their grandchildren in their retirement years.

Belief: All elderly are poor.

Reality: The poverty levels of the elderly are no different than those of younger age groups.[4]

Belief: There are continuous jokes about how older people are not good with technology.

Reality: A recent study found that 77% have a cell phone and 71% go online every day.[5]

Myths and stereotypes found to be *true* are that as we age, we are more dependable, wise, and kind. The reason is that as we get older, our oxytocin levels go up. Oxytocin is known as the "cuddle" hormone. Those with higher levels display more empathy, kindness, and generosity. These qualities need to be touted and appreciated.[6]

INVISIBLE OR INVINCIBLE

The negative myths and stereotypes are not global. There are wide ranges of attitudes about older citizens. Elders have been studied rather extensively.

In 2017, a collaborative study looked at the difference between attitudes and views on aging between the US, Japan, Mexico, and Lebanon. The researchers mapped the relationships with up to 20 of the closest people in the participants' lives. They were considered the inner circle (hard to imagine life without them), the middle circle (important), and the outer circle (not that close).[7]

The subjects also listed the top ten people in their networks.

There was one universal finding: children were the close and frequent supporters as they aged. Interestingly and not surprising, there were several country-specific findings. In America, participants reported having the largest social networks with an average of 11.3 close relationships. However, these networks got smaller with age.

In contrast, this did not occur for the Japanese and Mexican participants. The Lebanese social networks started out smaller (5.8 important relationships), and got larger as they aged.[8]

This shows that social networks do not shrink universally as they do here in the US. Another study looked at the health outcomes of Japanese and American groups based on social network structures. They identified four common network types: diverse (includes friends and family), friend focused, family focused, and restricted (isolated).

In Japan, the most common network type (29% of participants) was family focused. Married and widowed individuals had frequent contact with family members. In the US, 32% of participants reported living in a diverse network. This has been found to produce the highest state of well-being. Primarily, married participants interacted with a large network of friends and family. In the US, many negative networks were restrictive and provided little emotional support as well as the lowest sense of well-being.[9] Those reporting this had more depression and poor physical health.[10]

In contrast to America, when Japanese participants reported low support levels, it did not correlate with poor physical or mental health.

Researchers have found that as we age, our condition is often impacted by cultural stereotypes. When infirmity is expected, it often occurs. However, if these stereotypes are changed, people's conditions improve. In fact, researchers have discovered that when perceptions are changed and become more positive, people live an average 7.6 years longer than those with negative views. [11]

To show what happens when stereotypes change, in 2014, 100 adults in the US between 61 and 99 were studied. Participants were divided into four groups and followed for over eight weeks. One group was given flash words on a screen with positive stereotypes. They were described as "spry" and other positive words. Another group wrote short essays and had neutral words flashed on the screen. The third group wrote short essays and had positive words flashed. The control group had tasks related to clothing. At the end they all completed an image of aging scale and physical fitness survey. It went from helpless to capable. Those flashed the positive words had a 30% reduction in negative views of aging and were found to have improved physical functioning. [12]

In my own integrative medicine practice, I've had quite a few patients over the age of 80. They are amazing. One had been a powerful businesswoman who traveled the world. Another escaped east Berlin during World War II, and yet another worked on the Manhattan project (atom bomb) and was one of the last workers to remain alive. They all had incredible stories to tell. I decided to have a luncheon honoring them; a great affair., with over 20 people. They had so much fun talking and joking and swapping stories with each other. They all showed up on time, left on time and each wrote beautiful thank you notes. Homage to a bygone era. I am so glad I did that. Beyond the luncheon, I was able to be there for them and listen and appreciate who they were in each of our visits. I believe being respected and revered as well as truly being heard positively affected their well being and vibrancy more than any miracle pill I could prescribe.

Amazing what a positive attitude can do. Clearly, we need a cultural shift in how we treat our elders. This is something we all can promote by being our best selves and not falling prey to the negative stereotypes.

There is no need to be invisible.
Invincibility is ours for the taking.

10

INVINCIBILITY

In my opinion, invincibility is the ability to persevere and persist in the pursuit of our goals, even though others may try to dissuade us or stand in our way. It requires courage and confidence.

We often are treated like we don't know what we are talking about, which can cause us to doubt ourselves. That adds to the sense of invisibility, the feeling that we don't matter and neither do our beliefs. Many shrink from sharing their opinions and ideas. In fact, one survey found that 70% of older women feel this way(1). As we get older, we can do more than sit in a rocking chair and bake cookies!

As women, we have struggled with invisibility to some degree our entire lives. Fortunately, pioneers and role models like Ruth Bader Ginsburg have paved the way for us to become empowered and throw off that invisibility cloak, but it hasn't been easy. If you ask any woman about experiences of invisibility, I bet each will have many stories to recount. I can only speak for myself.

My life has been a lesson in how to beat it and achieve invincibility. I remember that as early as 6th grade, when a teacher pegged me as an "average" student. She told my mother I would make a good flight attendant one day. (Actually, at the time she said stewardess).

My mother was totally offended. She knew she was wrong (about the average part) and encouraged me to do my best. Fortunately, my seventh grade teacher was wonderful and realized that we all have potential. She encouraged me and told me I could do anything and, fortunately, that feeling stuck.

When I made it through high school and went to college, I decided to become a doctor. I was belittled and sneered at by my competitive male colleagues. They tried to box me into a corner. At that time there were very few women going into medicine. I had to find my inner strength, ignore them, and do what I needed to do. I studied hard and persevered. I was admitted to seven medical schools.

In medical school, my fellow female students and I had to work harder and be better than the men. Throughout my residency training in internal medicine, I had to fight to be seen and heard.

During my first rotation as an internal medicine resident at the Oregon Health Sciences University Hospital, I had an experience that exemplifies this. I was on call and received a female patient from the emergency room. The patient was being readmitted for abdominal pain after appendectomy surgery several weeks earlier. The appendix had been normal. She was operated on for abdominal pain, which had continuously gotten worse. No cause was found. (A bit of history: she had given birth several months prior to this, started birth control pills after the baby was born, and had been dieting to lose her baby fat.)

After speaking to her for quite a while and giving her a careful physical exam, I went to the library (no internet then!) to figure out what was going on. After several hours, I knew the answer. I went to her room, told her what I suspected and had her pee in a cup, stick it on the windowsill and wait for the sun to come up.

 INVISIBLE OR INVINCIBLE

When our team met in the morning for rounds, I presented my patient. I explained that she had abdominal pain which had worsened after adopting a low carbohydrate diet, taking hormones, and being exposed to anesthesia for her appendectomy. My diagnosis was *Acute Intermittent Porphyria*, a genetic condition caused by reduced levels of an enzyme called porphobilinogen deaminase. The lower levels are adequate until certain things activate it, such as hormones, drugs (anesthetics and pain meds) and low carbohydrate diets. When lower levels of the enzyme become overwhelmed, the chemical porphobilinogen builds up in the body *and* in the urine. Pain ensues. When the urine is exposed to sunlight, it turns a shade of purple.

The attending/supervising physician, to whom I presented the patient, did not make the diagnosis. I did. He told me I was wrong and refused to believe that the diagnosis was correct; even after we went in the patient's room and I showed him the purple urine in the cup. Even when I consulted with the porphyria expert at the University of Minnesota and *he* agreed with my diagnosis and sent me an experimental treatment for the patient called Hematin (no longer experimental), he refused to agree. Even after the patient's pain was finally relieved and diagnosis confirmed by the expert, he still refused to admit I was right. The important thing is that I knew it.

I stuck to my guns, and I gained confidence.
That is what I call invincibility!

The attending physician did not prevent me from my intention, which was to treat my patient with the best, most up-to-date therapy possible.

For a woman in medicine, as with any career, the quality of invincibility is important. I have been continually challenged. In my fellowship, as hard as I worked and as much as I accomplished, one of the senior people in my department had the audacity to introduce me to a visiting professor as "the secretary." That prompted a teachable moment for him. It was very hard for me to approach him. Part of me wanted to ignore the comment and quietly fade into the woodwork, become invisible, but I just couldn't let him get away with it.

I sat him down and expressed my dismay. I was furious but kept my cool. *Was* I invisible? Had he not seen me? Did he not appreciate what I had accomplished? I explained to him how insulting and demeaning that felt. I did not threaten legal action, however I did tell him that might happen if he did it again. I felt empowered and was able to move on in my career.

Eventually, I left academia and for many years worked in clinical internal medicine. I loved my patients and wanted to spend more time with them. Unfortunately, the clinic didn't agree. They wanted me to see patients in 10-minute increments. When I complained, they told me I was expendable. Basically, they were telling me I didn't matter. Once again, invisible.

One day, I found myself in a room talking to a patient, writing out multiple prescriptions, knowing that what the patient really needed was to be heard and not given more medications. Prescription writing was *not* why I went into medicine. I wanted to listen to my patients, figure out what was going on and help them heal.

I stepped off the office treadmill, left the clinic and decided to complete an integrative medicine fellowship with Dr. Andrew Weil at the University of Arizona. I redesigned a practice that worked for the patients and me. In my medical community, I was met with cynicism and negative comments. However, my

   INVISIBLE OR INVINCIBLE

practice became very successful, and I would say that about 80% of my patients are healthier as a result.

When I started my integrative medicine practice, I introduced a new, innovative fee-for-service model. I asked some of my colleagues to join me. They said it would never work. Dismissed yet again, I told them to watch me and sure enough, it was a successful model and others started doing the same, albeit ten years later.

I have found that, regardless of what I am doing, whether it is evaluating a patient, finding the best treatment for them, starting my own practice despite the naysayers, or pursuing media opportunities,

invincibility is important. Invisibility is not an option for me. Regardless of what field we are in or what we did during earlier adulthood, at this stage of our lives we have the wisdom, strength, and unapologetic "chutzpah" that age and experience has afforded us. Time to realize it, be proud and strut your stuff! You earned it. Be invincible.

PART THREE

INVINCIBILITY IN PRACTICE

11

JOY

OR

LIGHT YOURSELF UP FROM THE INSIDE OUT

Invincibility is not just about physical strength and wellness. It is also about mental health and wellbeing.

Finding the sweet spot for getting the most out of life is important. Joy is part of that, and it turns out, not that hard to find!

Joy is not discussed much in medical literature. Happiness is a huge topic, but joy is different. Happiness is something that occurs over time, joy is in the present.

Joy opens the heart and allows people to learn new skills more easily as well as help form very supportive relationships. Joy often results in harmony that makes this more likely. It gives a person a sense of being alive and energized. It is transcendent and freeing.

When people find themselves in a state of joy, they may notice a heightened state of awareness and that they are calmer. Time may fly by. When people are in a state of serene joy, time may slow down. Often people feel they are suspended in time.

It is important not to confuse joy with happiness. Happiness involves things that are often out of our control, in that they involve other people, such as marriage and work and family.

Joy is more immediate.

Things that can bring joy: walking out into the warmth of the sun, playing with puppies or being in a meadow or at the beach are all things you can do on your own. Joy lives in the moment and is easier to find. It brings us into the present.

Happiness can take you out of the present as it often involves reflecting on past experiences and goals.

Joy is in the now.

Studies have found that joy causes people to have a more open-minded view of the world. Joyful people attract others. Research shows that emotions are contagious. Joy is not only good for the soul but for the body as well. It lowers our daily cortisol, decreases inflammation and blood pressure. The experience of joy is contagious.

Joy opens us up to more joy.

This causes an upward spiral, something we rarely hear about.(1) We almost always hear about those downward spirals!

If joy improves our health and appearance, it opens us up to opportunities and favorable interactions. This fosters emotional resilience.

The good thing is that joy is easy to find.

One way to find it is to see it and take a picture of it! Scientists discovered that daily experiences of curiosity, joy, gratitude, and love can help a person find growth, success, and positive connections. However, only 20% of people may be finding joy; those who don't may be at risk of mental health problems. A study called *Picture This!* was designed to help people achieve joy(2). Subjects were asked to take two inspiring pictures a day for three weeks and focus on their emotional responses, because when we savor the moments, it brings us into that place of joy.

What can you do to bring joy into your life? It is quite simple.

Walk outside and find parts of nature you like; a tree or a flower or even a blade of grass. Take a picture and share and savor it.

Buy or make a wonderful cup of coffee and relax. Taste it, enjoy it.

Dance!

Play with your dog or, if you don't have a pet, go to the Humane Society and play with the animals.

Hang out with your children or grandchildren.

Watch an inspiring movie.

Laugh!

Take a nice hot bath or shower and savor it.

Being in the moment of regular routines can also bring you joy. Even washing the dishes can do it. Feel the warm water on your hands. Enjoy the soapy feeling and delight in the cleanliness of the dishes.

Buying modeling clay was one joyous thing I did. I have been making figurines. I am not very good as a sculptor but making the little figures and seeing them after they are formed has brought me joy, and made me happy.

As we get older, it is the little things that bring us joy. As we approach the latter half of our lives, these little things take on more importance.

12

DANCE! CREATE! HAVE FUN!

*Being 60 years and beyond does not mean
you have to stop learning and creating.*

To the contrary, most people have more time and flexibility and can consider what they *really* want to do when they grow up!

What we know from neuroscience is that the brain has an element of plasticity. No matter what age, you can learn and expand your brain. It can be learning how to paint, speaking a new language, or even starting a new business. It can even be athletic, such as taking up ballroom dancing. Creativity and the brain have been studied at Harvard University by Shelley H. Carson.[1] She says:

"These changes in the aging brain may make it ideally suited to accomplish work in a number of creative domains. So instead of promoting retirement at age 65, perhaps we as a society should be promoting transition at age 65: transition into a creative field where our growing resource of individuals with aging brains can preserve their wisdom in culturally valued works of art, music or writing."

Just because you are over 60 does not mean your creative juices are gone. Quite the opposite. Regardless of your age, you can use your brain in such a way that you can be your most productive and happiest self. The best way to capture the energy and enthusiasm you had when you were young is to tap into your creativity. I have noticed that as I have aged, I have become willing to go off in my own direction despite what people think. I closed my medical practice and only see patients on occasion if they are so complicated they need someone to stand back and look at the whole picture of their health issues. Diagnosing weird things is my specialty!

For me, it is again tapping into my creativity. Doing this has freed me up to pursue other endeavors. It is funny that people look at me as "retired" because I don't have a regular practice.

*I have given up trying to explain what I do.
I have transitioned, not retired.*

     INVISIBLE OR INVINCIBLE

I hope by telling you about my many activities that you will be inspired to consider searching out fun, creative outlets that appeal to you.

For me, creativity is life.

My Experience

When I was in college, an English teacher clearly did not like my writing. In fact, she told me to go into science and avoid anything that involved literature or writing. I have a rebellious streak and fortunately did not listen to her. I dipped my toe into the world of writing by reporting medical cases and then performing research and publishing papers in journals. After some success, I advanced to writing a children's book and two health books that have been somewhat successful. Now, I am here writing for you. I feel compelled to keep my creative juices flowing; it is stimulating and energizing. In addition, I have written and videoed a course for the *Great Courses*. It is like writing a book and performing the audiobook. Called *The Scientific Guide to Health and Happiness*, it was fun, inspiring, and challenging. I continue to write by providing articles for a local newspaper and multiple blogs.

Most of my free time has been devoted to exercise. I should say, a particular form of exercise, ballroom dance. When I was in grade school and high school, I took ballet lessons. The idea of partner dancing was so weird. The ballroom dance lessons in junior high school were horrible. I was totally turned off. The boys were awkward, and the steps were boxy. It just wasn't fun.

As I progressed to college and medical school, dance fell off my radar. It wasn't until I hit 55 years of age that I became interested. I was asked to join the Dancing with the Rogue Valley Stars event as a "star" to raise money for charity. I decided to try it again. I went to the first meeting of the cast and previewed the different types of dances. Argentine tango caught my eye. It was so passionate and strong. I chose that dance to learn. My partner was 20 years old and VERY patient. He was adept at other dances as well. I learned our choreographed piece and we came in Third place.

After the competition, I was hooked on dance and my partner taught me salsa, night club two step and west coast swing. For a while, west coast swing was my main focus and still is to some degree. Once I stopped seeing patients, I could devote more time to dance. I dance for 1-2 hours at least three times a week with my coach/partners, and I practice almost every day by myself. I have added cha-cha, rumba, and Lindy hop to the mix. Not only is it fun, it is creative.

I can dance both the role of the leader and the follower. Both roles can be creative, however, the lead has most of the creative potential.

The dance is a real brain stimulator, especially when the roles switch back and forth. Not only does my brain work better, but my fitness level has increased as a result.

As the world opens post-COVID, I will dance all over the country.

Dance has put a spring in my step, inspired me, and has the added benefit of keeping me fit and healthy.

Pursuing creative activities to keep your brain and body healthy is supported by science. In fact, studies of EEGs (electroencephalograms or brain wave tests) have found in older people that creativity increases the complexity of neural networks by activating them. In other words, your brain gets charged up.

     INVISIBLE OR INVINCIBLE

When it comes to your body, ballroom dance increases balance, bone health and helps prevent dementia. In a study published in the New England Journal of Medicine, researchers focused on a variety of activities of those between the ages of 75 and 85 years and found those who ballroom danced 2-3 times a week reduced their risk of dementia by 76%.[2]

MORE REASONS TO DANCE

This study is the one most quoted, but others confirm this. Frontiers in Aging Neuroscience published a study in 2010 that looked at people between 64 and 94 years.[3] A group they called Amateur Dancers (AD) (who had danced for years) were compared to a group who had never danced. The AD group received high scores in everyday competence. They lived independently, were mobile, social, healthy and generally content with their lives. This contrasted with the Never Dancers, who showed poor performance in life competence.

The researchers hypothesize that dancing has a direct effect on cerebral health.

A study by the Imperial College of London gives further credence to this. They noted a direct correlation between lack of dizziness and dancing. Dizziness and lack of balance are big problems as we age.

Looking at MRI scans, they found differences in the brain between dancers and non-dancers when it came to spinning, revealing that dancing spurred cerebral changes.

I experienced this myself. When I first started dancing, I would become dizzy and nauseated from turning. I had to take medication to stop myself from throwing up! After hours of practice and dance time, I no longer feel that way and can perform turn after turn without becoming dizzy.

Furthermore, and even more exciting, is the idea that dancing stimulates nerve growth factors. Without these growth factors, cells die. Scientists discovered that these growth factors circulate in the body and maintain normal body conditions. These factors help maintain nerve transmissions and allow for us to adapt to our environment, but they degrade over time. However...

dancing initiates continued stimulation of growth factors, allowing for improved cognitive and physical function leading to healthy aging.

Martial arts can provide similar benefits, but some can be particularly taxing on the body. Tai chi is a gentle form, safe and fun to do. It can improve balance and memory. However, it does not provide the same beneficial interpersonal contact and cues as ballroom dance.

13

DRESS THE WAY YOU WANT

As you get older, you don't have to stop caring about what you wear. I have seen that some do. This is where invisibility takes over. However, one thing that can bring joy is feeling good about what you are wearing. Show your individuality and creativity. Know your body type and what makes you feel good as well as comfortable. When considering what to wear, ask yourself if it looks like you and fits your personality. Have fun with it.

Once reaching 60, there are a few fashion rules you might want to follow. We tend to accumulate many different eras of clothes; some you'll want to give away to Goodwill or a consignment shop. These include: floor length floral print dresses, muumuus, ankle length A-line, unstructured skirts, elastic-waisted "mom" pants. Also, pass on unstructured suits or pants, oversized t-shirts, jumper-type dresses, and last but not least, ugly sweaters with embroidery or appliques.

When you rebuild your wardrobe, stick with one color. It is classy. Keep it simple.

Accessories are great, but again, keep it simple. When it comes to accessories, get trendy.

Jeans work, as well; just make them straight, or wide leg jeans. The low cut, super tight jeans probably are not going to work well. Spandex jeans are flattering.

Make sure to insert bold colors into your wardrobe.

Have a pair of tailored black pants with a little spandex. For skirts, A-line cuts slightly above or below the knee are classic.

Find comfortable shoes with a slight heel.

Pantsuits are a great style choice. They work for day or night. They are very flattering.

Add a couple of fitted t-shirts and tanks to wear under blazers, and you have everything you need.

IF YOU HAVE A STYLE THAT WORKS FOR YOU, STICK WITH IT.

The key is to flaunt what you have and feel good doing it. Some women do the hippie thing and others go the sophisticated route. As we get older most of us find that it is easier to be the real us and express it with what we wear.

WHAT ABOUT YOUR HAIR?

I have been reluctant to write about hair. Hair is a highly charged issue when it comes to women. For men, it is a lack of it!

Out of necessity during the pandemic, many women let their hair return to its natural state, meaning gray. For some it was liberating.

I have noticed that gray hair for others adds to their *invisibility*. Some people look at gray haired women as old ladies. But it doesn't have to be that way.

A great example is the former ambassador to Ukraine, Marie Yovanovitch. While ambassador, she had reddish hair in a short hairdo. I am not sure it did her any favors.

Recently I saw her on Late Night with Stephen Colbert. She looked amazing. Her hair was a silver gray, in a wonderful bob-like hairdo. It took years off her look. I also saw Emma Thompson when she appeared on his show. She had different shades of gray in her hair, and it looked fabulous! So, the trick to having gray hair as an *invincible* woman is to have a style that suits your look and a tone that works with your complexion. It might require a little make up to emphasize your beautiful facial features.

                                    INVISIBLE OR INVINCIBLE

14

KIDS, FAMILY, FRIENDS; WHERE DO I FIT?

We all know how important family and friends are when we are young. Once we get busy in our lives and careers, they may not seem as important. However, as we get older and reach retirement age, they become essential in many ways. Why? There are oh, so many reasons.

First, those who are more involved socially with family and friends live longer. Isolation and loneliness can be deadly. Regardless of your health, these relationships are crucial. They improve quantity as well as quality of life.

Those who are social also have a stronger immune system, which helps to prevent infections that commonly afflict the elderly. They are also less depressed and have a better mental attitude when they have close relationships with friends and family. When they are happy and busy with family, they also have better cognitive function than those who are not.[1]

Believe it or not, text messaging is a great way for seniors to communicate. My mother, who is well above 80, loves texting. She does it all the time and is able to keep in touch with her kids and grandkids. She likes to email, and I think it keeps her brain healthy.

She is also an avid FaceBook user. These modalities of communication were true lifesavers during the 2020-22 pandemic.

Regular phone calls and visits are another way to help us feel connected. I personally like good old-fashioned letters. There is nothing better than writing a letter of gratitude to someone you love. It makes them feel good and you feel even better![2]

As a baby boomer, I think it is important to talk about the "sandwich" generation. This is the group of people caught caring for aging parents *and* children or grandchildren. A research study in 2012 by the Pew Foundation found that this group feels constantly rushed. However, despite what you might guess, they feel happy and fulfilled.[3]

A study by Portland State University researchers noted that "sandwiched" working couples felt supported and appreciated. They found it was important that couples took time out for themselves. That was essential for well-being when it came to the caretakers.[4]

Another study of the sandwich generation looked at Baby Boomers (Born 1946-1964) and Generation X (1965-1980).[5] They compared the characteristics of the sandwich caregivers across both groups. The sandwich caregivers were classified as those who had at least one child living with them under 18 years of age and provided care to a parent or sick or disabled grandparent over the past 30 days. In this study, six percent of Baby Boomers and 31% of Generation X were sandwich caregivers. The Baby Boomers had less chronic health conditions and more mental distress. The Gen X group had more health conditions and less mental stress. However, both groups were in better health than other caregivers.

As we all continue to age, this sandwich generation phenomenon is growing. According to the US Bureau of the Census, the percentage of men between 25 and 34 years living at home with their parents rose from 14% in 2005 to 19% in 2011 and from 8% to 10% in women over the same period. Women are much more likely to be the care provider than men to the tune of 75% vs 25%.[6]

The good thing about caregiving for our loved ones is that it gives us a chance to remember the past and connect multiple generations. Pooling resources can be helpful, and property owned by our parents may increase in value, a plus for those living together.

The key is that caregivers recognize the importance of taking time off and caring for their own needs. Studies find that most "sandwiched" people are, indeed, relatively happy compared to those who are not. But, buried in that sandwich is a big dollop of self care!

FRIENDS

Having a group of friends is important. In Okinawa, Japan, where people live well past 100, people have groups of friends throughout life called moai who support each other and get together frequently. This is one of the reasons this group of people is happy and lives so long.

According to a Harvard research study, lack of social connections increased our chance of dying prematurely by 50%. In cultures where people help each other, there is a greater sense of meaning to life which helps them to be healthier and happier. When you have a group of friends or moai, you have a safety net and a tremendous amount of support.[7]

If you don't have a moai, you might find one by joining a group. Check out a book or dance club, martial arts studio, sports team, volunteer or community group.

The key is to find something you enjoy and are passionate about. Find your tribe, a health focused one, because healthy habits can be contagious.

One important key to a long life is to feel safe and cared for. Having a loving family is one way to feel that and having a group of friends who care for each other is priceless.

15

LET'S TALK ABOUT SEX

I guess it depends on how you look at it.

Research suggests that 40% of people aged 65 to 80 are sexually active. Great for that 40%! However, that means, 60% are not.[1]

That is unfortunate.

Sex is important for overall health and keeps people motivated to pursue a healthy lifestyle as well. Those with active sex lives are more likely to get regular checkups, take their medication and adopt healthy habits. They also have more confidence which adds to the feeling of invincibility. In terms of relationships, those with a healthy sex life tend to have a better bond.

Unfortunately, some people feel that sex has an expiration date. It doesn't and, in fact, can get better as we age.

A study of sexuality and senior health showed that having sex was something people wanted well past the age of 60. The sex may be different from that of teenagers, but it can be equally as exciting.

WHAT ABOUT VAGINAL DRYNESS?

There can be issues, but they can be dealt with. Once a woman goes through menopause, vaginal dryness can develop. It is extremely common. Having sexual intercourse can feel like you are being ripped apart. For this, I recommend a small amount of a weak form of estrogen called estriol, which works to build up the vaginal wall. It is inserted as a vaginal suppository every other night or nightly, if needed.

For women who prefer to avoid estrogen, vitamin E vaginal suppositories are very helpful. Carlson makes a good one. Just don't mix up the suppositories with their fish oil capsules…they kind of look the same. (Yuk, I know!) Using coconut oil or another vaginal lubricant during intercourse is also a good idea.

WHAT IF I AM NOT GOOD AT VAGINAL INSERTION?

I know I am not good at inserting things vaginally. An effective procedure, especially in the perimenopause period, is called the Mona Lisa Touch, particularly good for women who have had breast cancer and do not want any estrogen exposure.

It is an in-office procedure that utilizes a laser to resurface the vagina. It requires three treatments each six weeks apart with a yearly follow up. It has helped many women get back to where they were prior to menopause. It is important to find an experienced provider. I have had this procedure and I assure you, it works!

SEXUAL DYSFUNCTION

Men often deal with erectile dysfunction and women may have trouble achieving orgasm, for many reasons. It could be physical. Chronic disease and pain can make enjoyment impossible. Often medications can be a problem. Antidepressants are known to make orgasm difficult to achieve.

                                    INVISIBLE OR INVINCIBLE

For these patients, I have prescribed what I call "Scream Cream," a combination of Viagra, arginine, and aminophylline, all medications that open or dilate blood vessels. It is applied to the clitoral area 40 minutes prior to sexual intercourse and bingo, orgasm becomes much easier to achieve. I order it through a compounding pharmacy. It is a standard formula that can be prescribed by your doctor to a compounding pharmacy near you. There are no side effects and it is easy to use.

How did it get its name?

A patient of mine went to Hawaii with her husband. She had her vaginal estriol and Viagra cream in hand, so to speak. They had a great time. One night, they were engaged in sexual intercourse and it got quite loud and vocal. It was so loud that someone called security. Those listening were afraid someone was getting hurt.

Needless to say, my friends were quite embarrassed. We still giggle at the thought of this incident and marvel at how Scream Cream got its name!

What about desire?

When it comes to libido, the desire for sex, things get a bit more complicated. The reason for this is that we as women are very complex. It takes more than a look to get us going. Men are much easier to arouse.

Most women I interviewed and cared for told me that feeling loved, safe, and appreciated is what turned them on. A casual boob grab just doesn't cut it. I don't know how many men I have told, including my own husband, but they still don't quite understand!

A nice dinner, a compliment or two and a good conversation wherein a woman feels heard, can do the trick. The most powerful sex organ for a woman is her brain.

Feeling good helps, too!

To feel good, eating healthy and exercising also make a big difference. It is also important to avoid smoking and excessive alcohol.

Sex no longer needs to be rushed.

After menopause, pregnancy is no longer an issue. Many people over sixty are retired or winding down from busy jobs, so they have a bit more time. There is no need to rush, and exhaustion is not as much of a factor.

Talking is key

Talk about sex with your partner. Find out their level of interest and express yours. If things are not functioning the way you want them to, there are options. People giggle when you talk about sex toys, but they are readily available online and can help. Check out Amazon, there are tons and are delivered in discrete packages. No reason not to try them.

Masturbation is another option, with or without a partner. Contrary to the grade school nuns, who talked about the evils of masturbation, your hands won't fall off. It is good for you. It keeps everything in working order.

What about frequency?

How often do most people over 60 have sex when they are involved with a partner? Surveys say 22% have sex once a week. Twenty-eight percent have sex once a month. Thirty-nine percent say they want it more often.[2]

After all these years, can it still be good?

If you ask women over 60 in a committed relationship if sex is better now than when they were younger, they will tell you it is better now. They have learned to communicate better and know what works for them. For most women, enjoyment is more about the affection and closeness than the actual act of intercourse. Oxytocin, referred to as the love hormone, is released during sexual interactions. It helps with bonding and feeling close and lasts up to 48 hours after sexual intercourse.

WHAT ABOUT A NEW PARTNER?

If you are considering a sexual relationship with someone new, remember sexually transmitted illnesses are out there. You and your potential partner should be tested, and you need to talk about your past histories. This is very important since more seniors are having sex. As a result, the incidence of sexually transmitted infections is rising. A survey by the CDC found that the highest rises in those over 55 were in Washington D.C., New York, and Maryland. These diseases included Chlamydia, gonorrhea, syphilis, and HIV.[3]

Between 2008 and 2017, Montana saw an increase of 275.1%, the highest among any state in the country. Researchers fear that the increases will rise even higher since people were isolated and feeling lonely during the COVID -19 pandemic.

I don't want to close this chapter on a downer. Just be careful. And, if you are not happy with your sex life with a partner, there are special sex counselors available. You don't even need to go into their office. You can do the sessions online.

There is a great movie that is a good example of why it is important to understand your wants and needs and why it is important to talk about them. It is called, *Good Luck to You, Leo Grande*. Emma Thompson is the main character. She played a retired, widowed schoolteacher who wanted to experience the enjoyment of sex. She hired a young, handsome male "sex worker". They had an evolving relationship that allowed her sensuality and sexuality to emerge. It took a while, but when it did, she felt great about herself and declared she was invincible! (Of course, I loved that part!)

16

WHAT YOU NEED TO KNOW ABOUT SLEEP

It is hard to be invincible if you're dragging because you constantly feel tired. That is why it is so important to get a good, restful night of sleep.

We are still somewhat "in the dark" when it comes to knowing why we need sleep. We spend roughly a third of our lives sleeping. We do know that rest is important for growth, weight control and overall good physical health, and it is essential for good mental health.

A poor night's sleep can ruin your day. It turns out that certain parts of the brain that rule emotions (specifically the amygdala) can override the more logical part of the brain (the prefrontal cortex) when you are sleep deprived.[1] That helps explain why many are so emotional when exhausted, and why chronic sleep deprivation can lead to depression and anxiety.

WHAT IS HAPPENING?

There is a neurochemical produced in the brain known as adenosine, which governs our sleep-wake cycle. It builds up during the day and is cleaned away when we sleep. If we do not get adequate sleep, it sticks around and makes us feel foggy and groggy. Napping can help clear some of it, but a good night's sleep is really essential.

People who sleep less than 7–8 hours a night often have impaired memory and cognition. They are more prone to inattention and are more likely to have car accidents due to loss of focus. It is estimated that tired drivers are responsible for 50,000 injuries and 800 fatalities a year.[2]

How much sleep do we need?

Seven to eight hours is ideal for those over 65. It turns out that about a third of Americans sleep less than 6 hours a night. Fifty to seventy million people in the US suffer from chronic sleep disorders and we are not alone. Up to 30% of people around the world suffer from insomnia.[3]

What can we do?

The best place to start is by getting information. Are you getting enough sleep and are you getting enough of the good sleep? Sleep is made up of a variety of cycles. We know about REM sleep. It is talked and written about all the time. It is where we dream.

In addition to REM there is non-REM sleep. So many things go on at night while your eyes are closed!

What exactly is happening?

When you start to fall asleep, you are in non-REM stage 1, which lasts for minutes. Once the body relaxes, the brain waves slow. Light sleep ensues and is called Non-REM stage 2 where there is more brain wave slowing. This is when your body temperature drops and your muscles relax. Then you enter non-REM stage 3. This is deep sleep which happens early in the night and why you feel rested in the morning.

REM kicks in around 90 minutes after you fall asleep. It is called REM for the rapid eye movements that occur behind your lids. Brain waves look like those when you are awake. This is when you dream. Most people have two hours of REM a night. These cycles of Non-REM and REM sleep repeat all night long.

Why we dream is still not fully understood. It may be a way of cataloging and incorporating activities and experiences that occur during the day. Even though we may not completely understand why we dream, we do know it is essential.

                         INVISIBLE OR INVINCIBLE

For this reason, it is important to know what interferes with REM. One of the main interferences is alcohol. When you drink prior to falling asleep, REM is disrupted. Once the alcohol wears off in the middle of the night, REM starts up again and makes up for lost time. This often results in vivid dreams and nightmares.[4]

Interestingly, travel will also disrupt REM sleep. When we sleep in a hotel or an unfamiliar place, only half our brain sleeps. The other half is on alert. That may be a reason for not feeling as rested as usual when you are on a trip, in addition to jet lag which messes with our circadian or body rhythm.

So, I ask again, how do you know you are getting enough REM and Non-REM sleep?

There are Fitbits, special mattresses and Oura rings, all of which can tell you if you are getting the quantity and quality of sleep you need. They monitor your movements, heart rate, respirations, and body temperature. Some even offer advice on how to achieve better sleep.

GOOD SLEEP STARTS WITH GOOD HABITS!

Here are some tips for a good night's sleep:

Set a sleep schedule. Got to bed the same time every night and wake at the same time in the morning. Want to reset your clock? Camping is a good way to do that. You go to sleep when the sun goes down and rise when it comes back up!

Keep your room cool.

If you can, ban screens from your bedroom

Use your bed only for sex and sleeping

If you wake up in the middle of the night, rather than toss and turn, get up and meditate or read or listen to a relaxing story or calming app until you get sleepy

Exercise regularly

Avoid alcohol three hours prior to bedtime

Avoid eating at least two hours prior to bedtime

Avoid caffeine after 2 PM

If these tips don't help, you may have a sleeping disorder and it is time to see your doctor. You may be tempted to take a pill. As a physician who has been around a while, I urge patients to stay away from prescription sleep meds. They may help you sleep, but often it is not restorative sleep.

There are so many creative ways to improve sleep these days that it makes sense to try them before jumping to a pill. Hypnotherapy, Cognitive Behavioral Therapy, Relaxation Therapy and Meditation are techniques proven to help with sleep issues.

If you feel you need to take something, teas such as chamomile and an amino acid known as theanine can help relax you and get you to sleep. Theanine comes in many forms and is safe. There are other over the counter natural sleep remedies available. It is always a good idea to discuss these with your doctor before trying them.

17

Spirituality

Spirituality becomes important for many of us as we age. It particularly evolves as people develop chronic conditions, start to lose loved ones around them and deal with their own inevitable death. When someone feels connected and has a purpose, it is gratifying and comforting. It adds to their invincibility.

What is spirituality exactly? It is often connected to religion but really is more about a sense of purpose and meaning to life. Religion does not need to be a part of that. For some, it is being connected to a higher power. This can be the earth, nature, or God, or something entirely different. The concept is unique to the individual.

There are some differences between spirituality and religion. Spirituality is a broad concept that is informal and more of an inward experience. Religion is generally well-defined and formal, focused outside the individual and providing internal benefits.

Certain factors may prompt one to search for spirituality. Retirement is a big one; a time that can be uncomfortable and cause some to question their value without a job.

Loss is another major reason that people become more spiritual. It can help a person through the grieving process and guide them through the search for meaning in their own lives.

As some people get older, they lose independence. They may no longer be able to drive or move as they did. Spirituality can help the transition as someone becomes more dependent on others.

As people age, they generally find themselves with more time. This allows for reflection and the ability to make deeper connections to others.

Our own mortality stares us in the face as we age. Spirituality can help reduce the anxiety that may accompany our fears about death and dying.

All these reasons may help older individuals to focus inward. They may find themselves making meaningful connections and enjoying the ability to live in the moment.

WHAT ABOUT RELIGION?

Religion is important as people age. A survey done by the Pew Research Center in 2014 found that 85% of Americans over the age of 65 rated religion as very or somewhat important.[1]

Other beliefs they found in those over 65 were:

74% believe in heaven

70% believe in God with 100 percent certainty

65% said they pray at least once a day

56% said they believe in hell

48% said they attend religious services weekly.

What are the most popular religions in Americans over the age of 65?

83% identify as Christians, 24% as Catholics. Two percent described themselves as atheists and another 2% said they were agnostic.

THE POWER OF SPIRITUALITY

Spirituality has been correlated with improved outcomes and works well when combined with senior care. It can provide comfort, peace, and courage to those struggling with severe illness.

INVISIBLE OR INVINCIBLE

Adding spiritual counseling to a medical regimen can be incredibly helpful. It can restore relationships, improve a person's outlook, and offer hope and meaning.[2]

Knowing this, what can you do to add spirituality to your life? Religion offers spiritual practices. Praying, chanting, rituals, etc. are all part of that. However, finding something you love to do that makes you feel good can improve your spirit. Activities like volunteering, being out in nature, meditation, sharing stories and being part of a club such as a book club can be very beneficial. Dance and music help with feeling connected and bring joy.

Writing can help tremendously. Arts and crafts, creating something can also help with finding spirituality. Who knows? Your purpose may be to find the great artist or writer hiding in your soul.

Laura Ingalls Wilder, author of *Little House on the Prairie*, Bram Stoker author of *Dracula*, and Frank McCourt author of *Angela's Ashes*, all published their works when they were over 60! Grandma Moses did not start painting until she was 77 years old.

It is NEVER too late. Be daring. Be invincible.

Conclusion

I hope *Invisible or Invincible* has given you some ideas on how you can be your best, invincible self; that is, if you want to be invincible. Some people prefer invisibility and that is great if it is *their* choice.

If nothing else, I hope you can look at being over 60 as a door to a new and exciting life, one of freedom and excitement. In many ways, the idea of being old and invisible is just a state of mind.

A great quote comes from an interview with Clint Eastwood, who continues to act and be active at the young age of 91. He talked about a 95-year-old friend who looked and felt great. The friend was asked what his secret was. The answer, "I never let the old man in." Toby Keith wrote a song about it.

About aging, Clint Eastwood himself said,
"I don't look like I did at 20, so what?"

We can take a lesson from these quotes and realize we don't need to let the old lady in, either! And we aren't 20 anymore. So what? And thank goodness! Twenty wasn't so easy. I still remember my 20s.

Stay young at heart and be open to new experiences. Notice all the amazing people you have around you.

Be curious. It is incredible what you can learn and see.

When I was in medical school and early on in my career, being young and enthusiastic, I was most interested in the physical elements of a patient's medical history. As time went on, that became secondary to their social history, their real story. That is where I got to the root of most patients' problems. People are so interesting, if you listen to them!

It is astounding that more people don't listen. They love telling you about themselves and rarely engage the listener with questions. What a shame. They miss so much. For me, it is what makes life fun and interesting.

I have met so many fascinating people with incredible stories. One of my patients worked on the Manhattan Project (The making of the atom bomb). He was one of the few still alive. His story was one of intrigue and excitement and deep regret.

Another was one of the most respected handwriting analyzers in the country.

I had discussion with someone who was a young Jewish girl in Poland during WWII. She and her parents and sister stayed alive by train hopping. At one point they became so hungry that her father was willing to trade her sister for a bag of groceries to a German soldier. Her mother stopped him and saved her.

Another woman I met at a luncheon was in the French resistance during the war. She saved countless Jewish lives. We were waiting in line and chatting when someone cut in front of us. She laughed and said, "Let them cut in. Those things don't bother me!" She had perspective, for sure.

So many people, so many stories. One of the best was one I read in the medical journal the Annals of Internal Medicine. Here is the excerpt from the monthly column they publish *On Being a Doctor.*

This excerpt was called *"Curiosity" by Faith Fitzgerald.*[1]

"When I was a young attending at San Francisco General Hospital, morning rounds usually consisted of briefly going over the 15 or 20 patients admitted to the team the night before and then concentrating on the "interesting" ones.

I was righteous and was determined to teach the housestaff that there were no uninteresting patients, so I asked the resident to pick the dullest.

He chose an old woman admitted out of compassion because she had been evicted from her apartment and had nowhere else to go. She had no real medical history but was simply suffering from the depredations of antiquity and abandonment.

I led the protesting group of housestaff to her bedside. She was monosyllabic in her responses and gave a history of no substantive content. Nothing, it seemed, had ever really happened to her. She had lived a singularly unexciting life as a hotel maid. She could not even (or would not) tell stories of famous people caught in her hotel in awkward situations.

I was getting desperate; it did seem that this woman was truly uninteresting.

Finally, I asked her how long she had lived in San Francisco.

'Years and years,' she said.

Was she here for the earthquake?

'No,' she came after.

Where did she come from?

'Ireland.'

When did she come?

'1912.'

Had she ever been to a hospital before?

'Once.'

How did that happen?

Well, she had broken her arm.

How had she broken her arm?

'A trunk fell on it.'

'A trunk?'

'Yes.'

'What kind of trunk?'

'A steamer trunk.'

'How did that happen?'

'The boat lurched.'

'The boat?'

The boat that was carrying her to America.

'Why did the boat lurch?'

'It hit the iceberg.'

'Oh! What was the name of the boat?'

'The Titanic.'"

*If you don't ask and you are not curious, you are missing
so much! There is more joy and excitement to be had.
Don't miss it. Listen for it.*

Find what makes you happy and what you are passionate about.
It can be something as simple as walking in nature, caring for
grandchildren or who knows? Writing a symphony! Create, paint,
play. It could be that you become the new Grandma Moses.

*You just never know unless you try!
Go on, get out there and Be Invincible!*

Acknowledgments

I would like to acknowledge my husband for his patience during this writing project, my trusty dog Vegas who has kept me company throughout and my amazing mother who has been both an inspiration and a motivation for writing this book along with my patients and friends who have taught me the true meaning of invincibility.

My mission in life is not merely to survive, but to thrive, and to do so with some passion, some compassion, some humor, and some style.

– Maya Angelou

About the Author

D r. Robin Miller, an established author (*The Smart Woman's Guide to Midlife and Beyond, Kids Ask the Doctor,* and *Healed: Health and Wellness for the 21st Century*), has gathered the knowledge, insights and information offered in *Invisible or Invincible* over the course of 33 years of treating patients, using the principles of integrative medicine and personal experience.

Board certified in Internal Medicine, she trained as an Integrative Medicine Fellow at University of Arizona with Andrew Weil . She is currently Medical Director of Triune Integrative Medicine, a highly innovative, consultative, integrative medicine company in Medford, Oregon.

Dr. Miller is an Executive Advisory Board member for Sharecare, an interactive health and wellness website founded in conjunction with Oprah Winfrey and Jeff Arnold (Creator of *WebMD*). Robin is also a medical reporter and a regular correspondent for KOBI-TV NBC5, the NBC affiliate in Southern Oregon.

She writes a regular column for the Grants Pass *Courier* and can be heard on Jefferson Public Radio on her show, *Doctor to Doctor.*

Dr. Miller lives in southern Oregon with her husband and in her free time, when she isn't dancing, she tends to their vineyard known as Peter William Vineyard.

References

Introduction

1. Hamel, MB, 2008
2. Christenson, J.T., 1994
3. Rocca, WA, 2011
4. Wolters, FJ 2020
5. Graham, J, 2020
6. Trelease, F.,2021
7. Horn and Miller, 2008

Chapter 1

1. Manson, JE, 2013
2. Clark, JH, 2006
3. Clavel-Chapelon, F, 2015
4. Lobo, RA, 2013
5. Islam, S, 2009

Chapter 2

1. Hadnazy, A, 2010
2. Dallas, J, 2005
3. Toscano, S, 2005
4. BBC News, 2017
5. Ramirez, J, 2020
6. Wang, S, 2021
7. Chong, PP, 2019
8. Sullivan, M, 2021
9. Valles-Colomer, M, 2019
10. Opie, R.S., 2020
11. Segal, A, 2021
12. Park, SH, 2021
13. Doll, J, 2022
14. Clarke, S, 2012
15. Deppomier, C, 2019
16. Riviere, A, 2016
17. Zhang, Q, 2020
18. Vallance, HD, 2005
19. Ferrario, C., 2014
20. Yong, E., 2019
21. Adulrab, S, 2020

Chapter 3

1. Buettner, D, 2016
2. Einarson, TR, 2017
3. Peterson, K
4. Bello-Corral, L, 2018
5. Karstens, A 2019
6. Agnoli,C., 2018
7. Estruch, R , 2013
8. Martin-Pelaez, S, 2020
9. Kostoglou-Athanassiou, 2020
10. Schwingshackl, L, 2017
11. Toledo, E, 2015
12. Ljungberg, T, 2020

Chapter 4

1. Griffin, M, 2021
2. www.bluezones.com/about/history/2022
3. Comana, F, 2022
4. ADA, 2022

Chapter 5

1. Birukov, A, 2021

Chapter 6

1. Mayo, 2022
2. Plastic Surgery.org, 2022
3. Khatri, M, 2021
4. ASPS, 2018
5. Hollimon,N, 2022
6. Healthline, 2020
7. American Society of Plastic Surgeons, 2022
8. WebMD, 2022
9. Healthline.com, 2022
10. Wisco, L 2018
11. QWO.com, 2022
12. Cirino, A, 2022

Chapter 7

1,2. Stanford *New Map of Life*, 2021
3,4. Goldman, B, 2019
5. Goldman, B, 2021
6. Herz,J, 2017
7. Armitage, H, 2020
8. Yarnal, C. 2011

Chapter 9

1. Charles, S., 2010
2. Bergman, Y.S., 2020
3. Hurd, M., 2016
4. Burtless, G., 2019
5. Smith, A., 2014
6. Zak, P., 2022
7. Armstrong, K., 2020
8. Armstrong, K., 2020
9. Huffpost, 2017
10. Karasawa, M.,2011

11. Levy, B., 2014
12. Levy, B., 2014

Chapter 11

1. Johnson, M., 2019
2. McKee, L., 2019

Chapter 12

1. Powell, A, 2011
2. Verghese, J., 2003
3. Kattensroth, J, 2010

Chapter 14

1. Tan, J.H., 2019
2. AMADA, 2020
3. Van Kessel, D., 2020
4. Evans, K, 2016
5. Miyawaki, C 2020
6. Bernstein, R, 2011
7. Berkman, L 2019

Chapter 15

1. Morgan, D, 2022
2. Fletcher, J, 2022
3. Llata, E., 2021

Chapter 16

1. Goel, L, 2013
2. NSC, 2022
3. ASA, 2022
4. Laurence, E., 2021

Chapter 17

1. Pew, 2015
2. Puchalski, C, 2001

Conclusion

1. Fitzgerald, F., 1999

Appendix/Bibliography

ADA. "Blood Sugar and Exercise". 2022

https://www.diabetes.org/healthy-living/fitness/
getting-started-safely/blood-glucose-and-exercise

Adulrab, S, Al-Maweri, S, Halboub, E. "Ursodeoxycholic acid as a candidate therapeutic to alleviate and/or prevent COVID-19-associated cytokine storm" *Med Hypotheses*. 2020 Oct; 143.

Agnoli, Claudia *et al.* "Adherence to a Mediterranean diet and long-term changes in weight and waist circumference in the EPIC-Italy cohort." *Nutrition & Diabetes* vol. 8,1 22. 25 Apr. 2018

Alkadhi, Karim *et al.* "Neurobiological consequences of sleep deprivation." *Current Neuropharmacology* vol. 11,3 (2013): 231-49.

AMADA Senior Care: https://www.amadaseniorcare.com/2020/03/
the-importance-of-family-in-a-seniors-life/

American Sleep Association. "Sleep and Sleep Disorder Statistics" *ASA*, 2022

https://www.sleepassociation.org/about-sleep/sleep-statistics/

American Society of Plastic Surgeons. https://www.plasticsurgery.
org/cosmetic-procedures/dermal-fillers. 2022

American Society of Plastic Surgeons https://www.plasticsurgery.org/
cosmetic-procedures/microdermabrasion.2022

Armitage, H. "Ageotypes' provide window into how individuals age, Stanford study reports." *Stanford Medicine*, 2020

Armstrong, K. "How Age Magnifies Experience: Deconstructing Cross-Cultural Differences in Aging." *APS*, 2020

BBC News. "Trying the Hadza hunter-gatherer berry and porcupine diet." *BBC News Magazine*, 2017

Bello-Corral, L, Sanchez-Valdeon, L, Casadro-Verdejo, I. *et. al.* "The Influence of Nutrition in Alzheimer's Disease: Neuroinflammation and the Microbiome vs. Transmissible Prion." *Front Neurosci.* 2021; 15: 677777.

Bergman, Y, Palgi, Y.Ageism, "Personal and Others' Perceptions of Age Awareness, and Their Interactive Effect on Subjective Accelerated Aging." *Journal of Applied Gerontology.* 2020. 40:12, 1876-1880.

Berkman, L. "An active social life may help you live longer" *Harvard News*, 2019

Bernstein, R. "More Young Adults are Living in Their Parents' Home, Census Bureau Reports". *US Census Newsroom Archive*, 2011

Birukov, A., Cuadrat, R., Polemiti, E. *et al.* "Advanced glycation end-products, measured as skin autofluorescence, associate with vascular stiffness in diabetic, pre-diabetic and normoglycemic individuals: a cross-sectional study". *Cardiovasc Diabetol* **20**, 110 (2021).

Buettner, D "The Island where people forget to die" *Readers Digest*, 2016

Burtless, G. Despite scary headlines, America's elderly continues to prosper." Brookings Op-ed. 2019

Chang, P, Yarnal, C "The Longitudinal Association Between Playfulness and Resilience in Older Women Engaged in the Red Hat Society." *Journal of Leisure Research*, 2016. 48:3:210-227

Charles, Susan T, and Laura L Carstensen. "Social and emotional aging." *Annual review of psychology* vol. 61 (2010): 383-409.

Chong PP, Chin VK, Looi CY, Wong WF, Madhavan P, Yong VC. "The Microbiome and Irritable Bowel Syndrome - A Review on the Pathophysiology, Current Research and Future Therapy." *Front Microbiol.* 2019 Aug 13; 10:1870.

Christenson JT, Schmuziger M, Maurice J, Simonet F, Velebit V. "How safe is coronary bypass surgery in the elderly patient? Analysis of 111 patients aged 75 years or more and 2939 patients younger

     INVISIBLE OR INVINCIBLE

than 75 years undergoing coronary artery bypass grafting in a private hospital." *Coron Artery Dis.* 1994 Feb;5(2):169-74.

Cirino, E. Does Cool Sculpting Work? Healthline.com 2022

Clark, James H. "A critique of Women's Health Initiative Studies (2002-2006)." *Nuclear Receptor Signaling* vol. 4 e023. 30 Oct. 2006.

Clarke, Siobhan F et al. "The gut microbiota and its relationship to diet and obesity: new insights." *Gut microbes* vol. 3,3 (2012): 186-202.

Clavel-Chapelon, F. "The French E3N Cohort Study." *International Journal of Epidemiology"*, Volume 44, Issue 3, June 2015, Pages 801–809

Comana, F "Non-exercise activity thermogenesis: a neat approach to weight loss." *NASM*, 2022

Dallas, J. William Beaumont (1785-1853) "Experiments and Observations on gastric juice and the physiology of digestion, Plattsburgh 1883" *JR Coll Physicians Edinb* 2005: 35:39

Depommier, Clara *et al.* "Supplementation with Akkermansia muciniphila in overweight and obese human volunteers: a proof-of-concept exploratory study." *Nature medicine* vol. 25,7 (2019): 1096-1103. doi:10.1038/s41591-019-0495-2

Doll, J.P., Vazquez, J.F, Schaub, C. "Fecal Microbiota Transplantation (FMT) as an Adjunctive Therapy for Depression—Case Report" *Front. Psychiatry*, 2022

Einarson, Thomas R *et al.* "Prevalence of cardiovascular disease in type 2 diabetes: a systematic literature review of scientific evidence from across the world in 2007-2017." *Cardiovascular diabetology* vol. 17,1 83. 8 Jun. 2018

Estruch, R, Ros, E, Salas, J, *et al.* "Primary Prevention of Cardiovascular Disease with a Mediterranean Diet." *N Engl J Med* 2013; 368:1279-1290

Evans, Kiah L et al. "Working Sandwich Generation Women Utilize Strategies within and between Roles to Achieve Role Balance." *PloS One* vol. 11,6 e0157469. 15 Jun. 2016

Ferrario, Chiara *et al.* "Modulation of fecal Clostridiales bacteria and butyrate by probiotic intervention with Lactobacillus paracasei DG varies among healthy adults." *The Journal of Nutrition* vol. 144,11 (2014): 1787-96.

Fitzgerald, F T. "Curiosity." *Annals of Internal Medicine* vol. 130,1 (1999): 70-2.

Gallagher, G. "Everything You Want to Know About a Vampire Facelift." Healthline.com, 2020

Goldman, B. "Stanford scientists reliably predict people's age by measuring proteins in blood." *Stanford Medicine*, 2019

Goldman, B. "Study reveals immune driver of brain aging." *Stanford Medicine*, 2021

Graham, J "What The 2020s Have In Store For Aging Boomers." *KHN*, 2020

Griffin, R.M. "Myths About Exercise and Older Adults." *Compass by WebMD*, 2021

Hadnazy, A. "Think Twice: How the Gut's 'Second Brain' Influences Mood and Well-Being The emerging and surprising view of how the enteric nervous system in our bellies goes far beyond just processing the food we eat." *Scientific American*, 2010

Hamel MB, Toth M, Legedza A, Rosen MP. "Joint Replacement Surgery in Elderly Patients With Severe Osteoarthritis of the Hip or Knee: Decision Making, Postoperative Recovery, and Clinical Outcomes." *Arch Intern Med.* 2008;168(13):1430–1440.

Herz, J, Filiano, A, Smith, A. et. al. "Immunity Review: Myeloid Cells in the Central Nervous System." *Cell Press*, 2017

Hollimon, N. "Microneedling." *Radiance by WebMD*, 2022

Horn, J, Miller, R. *The Smart Woman's Guide to Midlife and Beyond.* New Harbinger, 2008

Huffpost. "7 Cultures that Celebrate Aging and Respect their Elders." *Huffpost*, 2017

Hurd, M, Rohwedder, S. "Living Longer, Working Longer." *Rand Blog*, 2016

Islam S *et al.* "Trend in incidence of osteoporosis-related fractures among 40- to 69-year-old women: Analysis of a large insurance claims database, 2000–2005." *Menopause* 2009 Jan/Feb; 16:77.

Karasawa, Mayumi *et al.* "Cultural perspectives on aging and well-being: a comparison of Japan and the United States." *International Journal of Aging & Human Development* vol. 73,1 (2011): 73-98.

Karstens, Aimee J *et al.* "Associations of the Mediterranean diet with cognitive and neuroimaging phenotypes of dementia in healthy older adults." *The American journal of clinical nutrition* vol. 109,2 (2019): 361-368.

Kattenstroth, Jan-Christoph *et al.* "Superior sensory, motor, and cognitive performance in elderly individuals with multi-year dancing activities." *Frontiers in aging neuroscience* vol. 2 31. 21 Jul. 2010

Klein, A. "Mediterranean diet delays Alzheimer's for three extra years." New Scientist, 2018

Kostoglou-Athanassiou, Ifigenia *et al.* "The Effect of Omega-3 Fatty Acids on Rheumatoid Arthritis." *Mediterranean Journal of Rheumatology* vol. 31,2 190-194. 30 Jun. 2020

Laurence, E. Sleep Doctors "Explain the Very Strange Ways That Alcohol Can Affect Your Dreams." *Well + Good*, 2021

Levy, Becca R et al. "Subliminal strengthening: improving older individuals' physical function over time with an implicit-age-stereotype intervention." *Psychological science* vol. 25,12 (2014): 2127-35.

Lindberg, S. "Thermage vs. Ultherapy". Healthline.com , 2021.

Ljungberg, Tina et al. "Evidence of the Importance of Dietary Habits Regarding Depressive Symptoms and Depression." *International Journal of Environmental Research and Public Health* vol. 17,5 1616. 2 Mar. 2020

Llata E., Cuffe, KM., Pichetti V., Braxton JR, *et al.*"Demographic, Behavioral, and Clinical Characteristics of Persons Seeking Care at Sexually Transmitted Disease Clinics-14 Sites, STD Surveillance Network, United States, 2010-2018". MMWR Surveill Summ 2021; 70 (No. SS-7): 1-20

Lobo, R. "Where Are We 10 Years After the Women's Health Initiative?" *The Journal of Clinical Endocrinology & Metabolism*, Volume 98, Issue 5, 1 May 2013, Pages 1771–1780

Manson JE, Chlebowski RT, Stefanick ML, Aragaki AK, *et al.* "Menopausal hormone therapy and health outcomes during the intervention and extended pos stopping phases of the Women's Health Initiative randomized trials." *JAMA*. 2013 Oct 2;310(13):1353-68. doi: 10.1001/jama.2013.278040.

Martín-Peláez, Sandra *et al.* "Mediterranean Diet Effects on Type 2 Diabetes Prevention, Disease Progression, and Related Mechanisms. A Review." *Nutrients* vol. 12,8 2236. 27 Jul. 2020

Matthew Kuan Johnson (2020) Joy: a review of the literature and suggestions for future directions, *The Journal of Positive Psychology*, 15:1

Mayo. "Botox Injections."

https://www.mayoclinic.org/tests-procedures/botox/about/ pac-20384658.2022

McKee, Laura G *et al.* "*Picture This! Bringing joy into Focus and Developing Healthy Habits of Mind*: Rationale, design, and implementation of a randomized control trial for young adults." *Contemporary Clinical Trials Communications* vol. 15 100391. 29 Jun. 2019

Miyawaki CE, Bouldin ED, Taylor CA, McGuire LC. "Baby Boomers as Caregivers: Results From the Behavioral Risk Factor Surveillance System in 44 States, the District of Columbia, and Puerto Rico, 2015–2017". *Prev Chronic Dis* 2020;17:200010.

Morgan, D. "Women's Health: Sex, Intimacy, and Menopause". National Poll on Healthy Aging, University of Michigan, 2022

National Safety Council. *Drivers are Falling Asleep Behind the Wheel.* 2022

Opie, R, Ball, K, Abbott, G, *et al.* "Adherence to the Australian dietary guidelines and development of depressive symptoms at 5 years follow-up amongst women in the READI cohort study. BMC, 2020

Park, Soo-Hyun *et al.* "Cognitive function improvement after fecal microbiota transplantation in Alzheimer's dementia patient: a case report." *Current Medical Research and Opinion* vol. 37,10 (2021): 1739-1744.

Paterson, K.E., Mynt, P.J., Jennings, A. et. al. "Mediterranean Diet Reduces Risk of Incident Stroke in a Population With Varying Cardiovascular Disease Risk Profiles." *Stroke*, 2018. 2018; 49:2415–2420

Pérez-Guisado, Joaquín et al. "Spanish Ketogenic Mediterranean Diet: a healthy cardiovascular diet for weight loss." *Nutrition journal* vol. 7 30. 26 Oct. 2008, doi:10.1186/1475-2891-7-30

Pew. "U.S. Public Becoming Less Religious". Pew Research. 2015 https://www.pewresearch.org/religion/religious-landscape-study/belief-in-god/

Potter, O. "Dementia Rates Are Falling In Europe And The Us And Experts Credit Decline Of Smoking Dementia Affects 850,000 People In The UK." *The Independent*, 2019

Powell, A. "Harnessing your creative brain" *Harvard Gazette*, 2011

Puchalski, C M. "The role of spirituality in health care." *Proceedings (Baylor University. Medical Center)* vol. 14,4 (2001): 352-7.

Ramirez, J, Guarner, F., Bustos, L, *et. al.* "Antibiotics as Major Disruptors of Gut Microbiota." *Front. Cell. Infect. Microbiol.* 2020

Rivière, Audrey *et al.* "Bifidobacteria and Butyrate-Producing Colon Bacteria: Importance and Strategies for Their Stimulation in the Human Gut." *Frontiers in microbiology* vol. 7 979. 28 Jun. 2016

Rocca, Walter A. *et al.* "Trends in the incidence and prevalence of Alzheimer's disease, dementia, and cognitive impairment in the United States." *Alzheimer's & Dementia : The Journal of the Alzheimer's Association* vol. 7,1 (2011): 80-93.

Schwingshackl, Lukas *et al.* "Adherence to Mediterranean Diet and Risk of Cancer: An Updated Systematic Review and Meta-Analysis." *Nutrients* vol. 9,10 1063. 26 Sep. 2017

Sullivan, M. "Can a Ketogenic Diet Reduce Alzheimer's Risks and Symptoms?" AARP. 2021

Smith, A. "Older Adults and Technology Use" Pew Research Center. 2014

Stanford Longevity. "NMOI Report: The New Map of Life". 2021

Tan, Jit Hui *et al.* "Happiness and Cognitive Impairment Among Older Adults: Investigating the Mediational Roles of Disability, Depression, Social Contact Frequency, and Loneliness." *International Journal of Environmental Research and Public health* vol. 16,24 4954. 6 Dec. 2019

Tehrani, K. "What you need to know about thread lifts". ASPS, 2018

Toledo E, Salas-Salvadó J, Donat-Vargas C, *et al.* Mediterranean Diet and Invasive Breast Cancer Risk Among Women at High Cardiovascular Risk in the PREDIMED Trial: A Randomized Clinical Trial. *JAMA Intern Med.* 2015;175(11):1752–1760.

Toscano, S. "Here's What Eating Only McDonald's for 10 Days Does to Your Gut." *Good Housekeeping*, 2005

Trelease, F. "Are You A Female Over 45? Guess What? You're Invisible." *Connecticut by the Numbers.* 2021

Vallance, H D *et al.* "Marked elevation in plasma trimethylamine -N-oxide (TMAO) in patients with mitochondrial disorders treated with oral l-carnitine" *Molecular genetics and metabolism reports* vol. 15 130-133. 3 May. 2018

Valles-Colomer, M., Falony, G., Darzi, Y. *et al.* The neuroactive potential of the human gut microbiota in quality of life and depression. *Nat Microbiol* **4,** 623–632 (2019).

Van Kessel, P. "How Americans feel about the satisfactions and stresses of modern life" *Pew Research Review*, 2020

Wang, Shuang *et al.* "*Fusobacterium nucleatum*Acts as a Pro-carcinogenic Bacterium in Colorectal Cancer: From Association to Causality." *Frontiers in cell and developmental biology* vol. 9 710165. 20 Aug. 2021,

WebMD, "Laser Resurfacing." *Radiance by WebMD.*

Wisco, L Kybella: "Injectable Double Chin Reduction". 2018, *Healthline.*

Xue, L. Yang, X, Tong, Q, *et.al.* Fecal microbiota transplantation therapy for Parkinson's disease, Medicine: August 2020: 99:35 p 22035

Wang, Shuang *et al.* "*Fusobacterium nucleatum*Acts as a Pro-carcinogenic Bacterium in Colorectal Cancer: From Association to Causality." *Frontiers in cell and developmental biology* vol. 9 710165. 20 Aug. 2021,

WebMD . "What to Know about Kybella Injections." *Radiance by WebMD*, 2021

Yarnal: https://files.eric.ed.gov/fulltext/EJ985548.pdf

Yong,E. "Why are your gut microbes different from Mine?" *The Atlantic*, 2016

Zak, PP. "Oxytocin Increases With Age and Life Satisfaction and Prosocial Behaviors." *Front. Behav. Neurosci.*, 2022

Zhang, Qi, and Nan Hu. "Effects of Metformin on the Gut Microbiota in Obesity and Type 2 Diabetes Mellitus." *Diabetes, Metabolic Syndrome and Obesity: Targets and Therapy* vol. 13 5003-5014. 16 Dec. 2020